The Graying of the Flock

The Graying of the Flock

A New Model for Ministry

James L. Knapp

LEAFWOOD
PUBLISHERS

To the "Pillars of Faith" in my life

Chelsea and Gaynelle Reed

& Harry and Marian Knapp

Acknowledgements

Many individuals have contributed to the development of this book. First, and foremost, are the hundreds of church leaders who have given of their time and knowledge by completing a survey or being interviewed on the telephone or in person. I am deeply appreciative of your generosity.

Second, Southeastern Oklahoma State University has played a significant role by providing financial support through multiple Faculty Research Grants. In addition, the services of several student research assistants have proven to be invaluable. A sincere "thank you" is extended to Dr. Jack Robinson, Dr. Doug McMillan, Lisa Beaver, Toni Reed, Nancy Savage, Kristi Gourd, and Stephanie Sloan.

Finally, I am deeply indebted to my wife Tracy, who patiently listened as I wrestled with the manuscript and gently offered suggestions on how to improve it. Tracy, your love and support are priceless.

James L. Knapp

Table of Contents

One

The Demographic Shift

The United States is in the midst of a dramatic transformation. Our population is aging at such a rapid rate that, recently, we passed a major milestone. For the first time in the history of our nation, there are more senior citizens than teenagers.[1] Other statements concerning the age distribution in the United States tell the same story. For example:

- Americans over the age of 65 are the fastest growing segment of the population.[2]
- The population over the age of 65 is increasing twice as fast as the population as a whole.[3]
- Between 1960-1990, the number of individuals over the age of 85 increased 232%.[4]
- The number of individuals over the age of 100 has doubled in the last ten years.[5]

All of this information points to one clear conclusion: we live in an aging society. However, in spite of all that has been spoken and written about the aging of the American population, the reality is that we are only experiencing the tip of the iceberg. The full impact of the aging of the population is yet to come. As in other industrialized nations, several social and medical factors came together in the United States during the twentieth century to produce an unprecedented "age wave"[6] that is reshaping the way Americans think about aging and the elderly.

In this chapter we will explore the factors that have contributed to the graying of the population and the societal response to it. We will also focus specifically on how religious groups are responding to the "age wave."

A Century of Increase and Innovation

Between 1900 and 1999 life expectancy in the United States increased by nearly 30 years![7] On average a person born in the United States at the beginning of the twentieth century could expect to live 47 years. By the close of the twentieth century, a typical American could expect to live 75 years.

The extension of life expectancy did not occur by accident. During the century, a number of scientific discoveries and technological advancements made significant contributions to increasing life expectancy. For instance, at the beginning of the century indoor plumbing, refrigeration, penicillin (and, subsequently, antibiotics), and automobiles were either completely unknown to Americans or available only to the most privileged individuals. By 1999 these items were considered necessities by the overwhelming majority of Americans.

These improvements have been important to extending

life expectancy, but they provide only a partial explanation for the aging of the population. The second major factor is the "baby-boom" generation. It is not uncommon for a "baby-boom" to occur following a war. A careful examination of the years immediately following major conflicts involving the United States reveals that several "baby-booms" have occurred. However, the one that followed World War II was unique. Between 1946 and 1964, 76 million babies were born. In contrast, between 1965-1983, only 66 million babies were born.[8] The noticeably smaller "baby-bust" generation not only highlights the enormous size of the "baby-boom" generation but will also be a major contributor to the changing demographics of the twenty-first century.

As the "boomers" have moved through the life cycle, they have transformed every stage along the way. When

Figure 1
"Boomers" vs. "Busters"

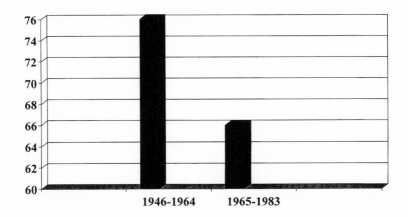

they were infants, baby food and diaper companies thrived. When they started school, primary and secondary schools were forced to expand. As teenagers and young adults, they provided the majority of the manpower for the Vietnam War and the counterculture movement of the 1960s. College and university campuses were filled beyond capacity during the 1960s and 1970s due, in part, to the deferment from military service that college enrollment provided. The "boomers" used their college educations to enter the workforce during the 1970s and 1980s and to move gradually upward in their chosen professions so that by the 1990s, members of the "baby-boom" generation were occupying significant leadership positions throughout American society. At the beginning of the twenty-first century, "boomers" range in age from the mid-30s to the mid-50s and are rapidly approaching the threshold of retirement.

The Importance of 2011

Taken together, the increase in life expectancy and the overwhelming size of the "baby-boom" generation is providing the major impetus for the graying of the population. As mentioned previously, though, the full impact of the "age wave" is yet to come. Currently, 13% of the American population is 65 years of age or older.[9] But that percentage will expand steadily. The first wave of the "baby-boom" generation (individuals born in 1946) will reach the age of 65 in the year 2011. Every year after that, another wave of "boomers" will reach age 65 until the year 2029. By the year 2030, the entire "baby-boom" generation will have passed the age that traditionally has

Figure 2
Percent of Americans Over the Age of 65

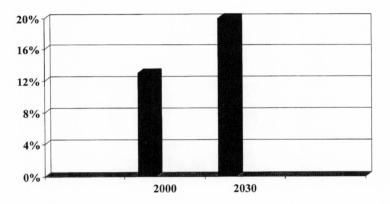

designated the entry into old age. At that time, 20% of the American population will be 65 years of age or older![10] In other words, one out of every five Americans will be "elderly." Of course by that time, the age at which a person is considered to be "old" may very well have changed. Indeed, based on the boomers size, education, wealth, and work experience, it is quite probable that they will change the face of retirement just as they have revolutionized the earlier phases of the life cycle.

Aging Within the Church

Many Protestant churches have been experiencing a graying of their memberships for several years due to at least two reasons. First, increased life expectancy has allowed more individuals to maintain their religious

Figure 3
Percent of Congregation Over the Age of 65

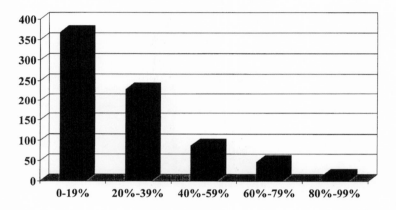

involvement well into their 70s, 80s, and even 90s. Second, as members of the "baby-boom" generation have moved into their late 40s and early to mid 50s, they have begun to push the average age of the typical congregation higher.

In my first study, I asked 754 pulpit ministers to estimate the percentage of their congregation that was 65 years of age or older. The greatest number of responses fell in the "0-19%" category which is an indication that the membership in the local church is very similar to society at large. I also asked each pulpit minister to estimate the percentage of his congregation that was 55 or older. The responses clearly show the presence of the "baby-boom" generation and reinforce the earlier comments about the

Figure 4
Percent of Congregation Over the Age of 55

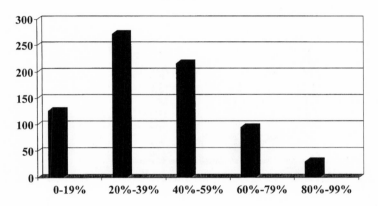

"boomers" looming on the horizon. In a typical congregation, anywhere from 20%-40% of the members are 55 years of age or older.

In my subsequent research, I studied several different Protestant churches and was astounded at the results. In an average congregation, 23% of the members are 65 years of age or older.[11] In other words, nearly one in four members have reached or exceeded their mid 60s. Keep in mind that 22% is the average. In some congregations, the figure is much higher. In fact, some respondents indicated that 40%, 50%, or even 60% of their members were 65 years of age or older.

For many, this information could be interpreted as bad news and seen as an indication that churches are slowly dying. Another interpretation of the data, however, is far

Figure 5
Percentage of Church Over
the Age of 65

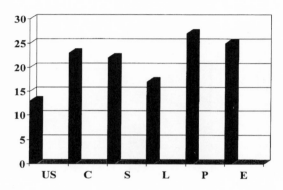

US – United States
C – Church of Christ
S – Southern Baptist
L – Lutheran
P – Presbyterian
E - Episcopalian

more optimistic. Many churches are in the early stages of a wonderful opportunity for ministry with senior adults. Not only are there more senior adults today than in the past, but as a group they are healthier, more active, and better educated than ever before. Far from being a liability to a church, senior adults are rapidly becoming one of the greatest assets a congregation can have. Fully utilizing that potential of senior adults, however, depends on adopting a new model of senior adult ministry.

The Basis of a New Model

Several years ago Oldsmobile recognized that it had an image problem. Sales of popular Oldsmobile cars were declining and the new styles being introduced were not appealing to consumers. Faced with a growing crisis, Oldsmobile attempted to change its image with an innovative advertising campaign. Using the adult children of several celebrities from the 1950s and 1960s, Oldsmobile extolled the virtues of its new line of vehicles while showing beautiful and exciting scenery in the background. At the close of the commercial, the celebrity's son or daughter was shown driving the car and the campaign slogan, "This is NOT your father's Oldsmobile," was presented. Unfortunately, Oldsmobile's efforts were not successful and the company has stopped manufacturing cars.

The story of Oldsmobile provides a penetrating example of what can happen when we do not recognize the changing nature of our surroundings. Oldsmobile continued to use an outdated model of business and failed to recognize that the wants, needs, and interests of their consumers had changed. By the time they responded to what was happening, it was too late.

A similar situation can happen in a local church. As large numbers of members move through the stages of the life cycle, new opportunities for ministry emerge. It is not a coincidence that youth ministries appeared in large numbers during the 1960s and 1970s. This was the era in which a sizeable portion of the "baby-boom" generation was in its formative years. Church leaders around the country recognized the need, and opportunity, for the local church to assist in developing a strong Christian presence in the lives of teenagers. Even after the "boomers" had moved through this phase of the life cycle, youth ministry had become so popular that it is now a fixture in many congregations. A similar process has occurred with campus ministry, singles ministry, and small group ministry. Each of these important ministry efforts has grown in response to the movement of the "boomers" through the life cycle. As members of the "baby-boom" generation draw closer and closer to what, historically, has been considered the age of retirement, new and exciting opportunities for ministry are emerging for congregations that are willing to embrace a new way of thinking about senior adults.

Adopting the New Model

Gerontology is an academic discipline that focuses on the biological, social, psychological, and economic changes that accompany the middle and later years of life. Within gerontology, two distinct theories have dominated the field. Disengagement theory suggests that as individuals become older, it is most beneficial to society for them to voluntarily withdraw from active involvement in meaningful social roles.[12] Retiring from full-time employment and stepping down from leadership roles in church and civic groups are but a few of the ways a person can disengage from society and open new opportunities for younger individuals. Not surprisingly, disengagement theory was introduced in 1961 when the "baby-boom" generation was still developing.

Today most gerontologists strongly oppose disengagement theory. Instead, they rely heavily on activity theory that stresses the societal benefits that accompany older individuals remaining active in meaningful social roles. For example, when a person retires from full-time employment, he or she can remain active by engaging in volunteer work, enrolling in college or continuing education courses, or pursuing a new or lifelong hobby. Activity theory does not specify the type of activity in which older individuals should participate. Instead, it simply encourages older individuals to continue to use their talents in ways that are meaningful to them and to those around them.

The new model for senior adult ministry rests squarely within activity theory. In the past, senior adult ministry typically meant ministry TO older individuals. Lower life expectancy and a less advanced health care system usually meant that individuals who survived into their seventh and eighth decade of life were not only extremely rare but also very limited in their mobility. Today, however, senior adults are healthier and more active than ever before. As a result, senior adult ministry is increasingly becoming ministry WITH, and in many cases ministry BY, older individuals. A growing number of congregations around the country are recognizing the time, energy, wisdom, and experience of their senior adult members and are searching for ways to harness it into meaningful ministry opportunities.[13]

As we will see in the remainder of this book, senior adult ministry can take place in a variety of innovative forms. Before discussing them, however, we must first address the primary question that should guide all ministerial efforts: "What has the Lord said about this"? In Chapter 2 we will focus our attention on Biblical mandates and precedents.

Two

Biblical Mandates and Precedents

Regardless of the specifics of a ministry program, Scripture is abundantly clear that without the Lord's blessing, human efforts are futile. With this in mind, it is imperative that every ministry undertaken by a church be in accordance with the will of the Lord. Based on this fundamental principle, our purpose in this chapter is to examine the Scriptures in order to gain an understanding of the Lord's will as it applies to senior adults and ministry with them. We will begin with a study of the terms used to describe senior adults.[1] Next, we will examine the lives of several Biblical characters who were active servants even in their later years. Finally, we will consider the significance of intergenerational relationships among the Lord's people.

"Aging," "Elderly," and "Senior"

The terms "aging," "elderly," and "senior" appear a total of two times in the Old and New Testaments. "Aging" and "elderly" each appear once and "senior" is not used at all. In Hebrews 8, the writer is discussing the first and second covenants and the superiority of the new covenant. In verse thirteen, the term "aging" appears but not in reference to an older person or the elderly in general. Rather, the writer states that the old covenant is obsolete and aging and that it will soon disappear.

The term "elderly" only appears once in the Scriptures but unlike the term "aging," it is in direct reference to older individuals. Leviticus 19 is in the middle of a lengthy section of Scripture in which the Lord is delivering the Law to Moses who will then present it to the children of Israel. In verse 32 the Lord instructs the people to stand in the presence of the aged and to show respect for the elderly. Interestingly, verse 32 ends with the phrase, "and revere your God." It appears that the Lord is emphasizing that by showing respect for the elderly we are also showing respect to God. This is an especially significant passage in 21st century America due to the gradual erosion of status that the elderly have experienced in our society.

"Old," "Older," and "Aged"

In contrast to the previous terms, the words "old," "older," and "aged" appear quite frequently in the Scriptures. By far the most frequently used of the terms is "old." Appearing more than 300 times, "old" is used predominately to describe either an individual's age or the age of an animal to be sacrificed. For instance, Genesis 25:8 describes Abraham as an "old man" who died at a "good old age."[2] And the book of Leviticus gives instructions regarding how old animals sacrificed to the Lord were to be.

The term "older" appears 32 times in the Bible. In at least three New Testament passages, principles of behavior are linked to a person's chronological age.[3] In 1 Timothy 5:1-2 and 1 Peter 5:5, younger individuals are instructed to "not rebuke an older man harshly" and to "be submissive to those who are older." In Titus 2:2 older men are instructed to "be temperate, worthy of respect, self-controlled, and sound in faith, in love, and in endurance." In Titus 2:3 older women are told to "be reverent in the way they live, not to be slanderous or addicted to much wine, but to teach what is good." These verses emphasize that younger people have the responsibility of treating older people with respect based purely on their chronological age.[4] At the same time, however, older people have the responsibility of living in accordance with God's will and providing a positive example of a life dedicated to the Lord.

"Aged" can be found eleven times in the Scriptures. Interestingly, the term only appears in the Old Testament. In addition to be being used to describe an individual's chronological position in the life cycle, such as Joseph asking about his aged father (Gen. 43:27), the term "aged" is also connected to certain attributes. In response to his friend Zophar, Job indicates that wisdom is found among the aged and that long life brings understanding (12:12). As the book progresses, however, the wisdom and understanding that Job had accumulated begins to wane and he seeks to justify himself rather than God. At that point, a younger man named Elihu comes to Job with a strong message: "I am young in years, and you are old; that is why I was fearful, not daring to tell you what I know. I thought, "Age should speak; advanced years should teach wisdom". But it is the spirit in a man, the breath of the Almighty, that gives him understanding. It is not only the aged who understand what is right" (Job 32:6-9).

When combined with the New Testament passages from 1 Timothy, 1 Peter, and Titus, Elihu's message to Job provides an important statement to Christians today. Older individuals are to be respected simply because they are older. However, advanced chronological age is not a guarantee of wisdom. The powerful presence of the Lord's Spirit in the life of a believer of any age is the source from which wisdom comes. An older person who has allowed the flame of the Spirit to grow dim must still be respected but will be very limited in his or her ability to exhibit biblical wisdom. The importance of maintaining an active, growing relationship with the Lord, even in our advanced years, is clearly highlighted in the passage from Job.

Biblical Characters

The Bible records many examples of people who remained active servants of the Lord even in their later years. Abraham, Moses, David, and the Apostle John are some of the earliest examples of senior adults who remained active in serving the Lord. Even though the manner in which they served was different from their earlier years, they continued to follow the will of the Lord and to be in service to Him. Beyond these individuals, there are four other biblical characters whose exemplary faith in their later years is also recorded in Scripture.

Having succeeded Moses as the leader of the children of Israel, Joshua led God's people across the Jordan River and into the promised land. With the help of the Lord, Joshua and the children of Israel had conquered Jericho and taken possession of a sizeable portion of the land of Canaan. However, late in Joshua's life, the process of claiming the entire promised land was not complete. As a result, the Lord spoke to him saying, "When Joshua was old and well advanced in years, the Lord said to Him, You are very old, and there are still very large areas of land to be taken over" (Josh. 13:1). The Lord recognized that the process of conquering the promised land was not complete and that Joshua was getting old. He also recognized that, despite Joshua's age, he was still capable of serving as the leader of the children of Israel. As a result, the Lord delivered instructions to him regarding how the remaining lands were to be divided.

Joshua's fellow spy, Caleb, is a second example of an older person who remained active in his service to the Lord. In Joshua 14 Caleb approached Joshua and asked for the inheritance of land that Moses had promised to him. Even as an older man Caleb's passion and conviction was still apparent. Joshua 14:10-12 says: "Now then, just as the Lord promised, he has kept me alive for forty-five years since the time he said this to Moses, while Israel moved about in the desert. So here I am today, eighty-five years old! I am still as strong today as the day Moses sent me out; I'm just as vigorous to go out to battle now as I was then. Now give me this hill country that the Lord promised me that day." Clearly Caleb did not disengage himself from meaningful social roles. He maintained an active faith in the promises given by the Lord and remained willing to use his talents in service to Him.

The third and fourth examples are found in Luke 2. Simeon and Anna were older persons waiting for the coming of the Messiah. Very little detail is provided about either of them but it is clear from their brief appearance in Scripture that they were faithful servants. In only three verses we gain a clear understanding of the depth of Simeon's faith. In verse 25 the Bible says that Simeon was a devout man and that "the Holy Spirit was upon him." Verse 26 says, "It had been revealed to him by the Holy Spirit that he would not die before he had seen the Lord's Christ." In verse 27 Simeon goes into the temple courts after being "moved by the Spirit." Clearly, Simeon was a Spirit-filled believer who responded to the will of the Lord even in his later years.

In verses 36-37 Anna is described as a prophetess who was very old. She had been a widow for a number of years and had dedicated herself to prayer and fasting in the temple. Like Simeon, seeing the Messiah was the culmination of a life dedicated to serving the Lord. Even in her later years, Anna had remained active in her commitment to God.

Intergenerational Relationships

An intergenerational relationship is one in which at least two individuals from different age groups come together for the purpose of sharing life experiences, learning from each other, and creating a mutually beneficial bond that transcends chronological age. A careful examination of Scripture reveals that the term "intergenerational" does not appear. However, the concept of intergenerational relationships is found throughout the Bible.

In Exodus 12 the Lord initiated the Passover and the Feast of Unleavened Bread. In verse 17 the Lord instructed the children of Israel to "celebrate this day as a lasting ordinance for the generations to come." In verse 26 Moses says, "And when your children ask you, 'What does this ceremony mean to you?' then tell them, 'It is the Passover sacrifice to the Lord, who passed over the houses of the Israelites in Egypt and spared our homes when he struck down the Egyptians.'"

The Passover was to become an important part of the heritage of the Israelites and the Feast of Unleavened Bread was to serve as a yearly reminder of what the Lord had done for His people. As time passed the Feast of Unleavened Bread would become even more important because it would connect future generations of Israelites to their physical and spiritual ancestors and to the awesome power of the God they served.

A related example is found in Deuteronomy 6. After wandering in the desert for forty years, the children of Israel were about to enter the promised land. Before crossing the Jordan River, however, Moses reminded the people of their heritage, the covenant God had made with them, and the laws He had decreed. As a part of his speech, Moses included the admonition found in verses 20-21: "In the future, when your son asks you, 'What is the meaning of the stipulations, decrees and laws the Lord our God has commanded you?' tell him: 'We were slaves of Pharaoh in Egypt, but the Lord brought us out of Egypt with a mighty hand." Moses understood the necessity of one generation communicating with another generation in order to ensure the continuation of their heritage and beliefs.

The Bible also includes two examples of intergenerational relationships that are more personal in nature. The short, Old Testament book of Ruth presents the development of an intergenerational bond between a mother-in-law and her daughter-in-law. The mutual love and respect the two women have for each other is very apparent as Ruth leaves her native country of Moab in order to return to Bethlehem with Naomi. Once there, Naomi shares information with Ruth about her family and the customs of the area. In return, Ruth shares with Naomi the grain she is able to gather, information from her daily activities, and listens to Naomi's advice regarding Boaz. Throughout the four chapters of the book, Naomi and Ruth share the happy, sad, and challenging times of their lives in such a way that a strong intergenerational relationship develops between them.

The friendship of Paul and Timothy provides another example of a strong intergenerational bond. Paul was first introduced to Timothy while on a missionary trip with Silas. As recorded in Acts 16:1-3, Paul was so impressed with young Timothy that he took him on the remainder of the journey. Paul continued to mentor Timothy and by the time 1 and 2 Timothy were written, Paul referred to Timothy as "my true son in the faith" (1 Tim. 1:2) and "my dear son" (2 Tim. 1:2).

A Biblical Model

All of the Scriptures mentioned previously lend support to the idea of a new model for senior adult ministry. However, 1 Corinthians 12 provides the strongest statement. Beginning in verse 12, Paul writes: "The body is a unit, though it is made up of many parts; and though all its parts are many, they form one body. So it is with Christ." Paul continues in verses 21-23: "The eye cannot say to the hand, 'I don't need you!' And the head cannot say to the feet, 'I don't need you!' On the contrary, those parts of the body that seem to be weaker are indispensable, and the parts that we think are less honorable we treat with special honor."

The message from 1 Corinthians is quite clear. Every member of the Lord's Body is important! Regardless of our chronological age, each one of us has been given a gift from God that is to be used to further the Kingdom. Nowhere in Scripture are Christians given permission to disengage from service simply because they are older. We are to continue serving the Lord, in whatever capacity our physical condition allows, until we pass from this life.[5]

Thus, not only is the new model for senior adult ministry necessary given the changing demographics, it is also extremely biblical. Ministry WITH senior adults taps into an abundant source of individual talents and provides an opportunity for older members of a church to remain active in their service to the Lord. A church that fully utilizes the gifts of their senior adult members for the good of the entire congregation will reap the bountiful harvest of wisdom that can only come from life experience. The challenge that most congregations face, however, is creating an environment that encourages the new model. In Chapter 3 we consider the fundamental issues of establishing a viable senior adult ministry.

Three

The Basics of
Senior Adult Ministry

Senior adult ministry is a relatively new idea. In the past, ministry efforts designed for youth, single professionals, and young families were far more prevalent due to the demographic composition of most congregations. Increasingly, though, congregations are experiencing the demographic shift described in Chapter 1 and are searching for ways to initiate or refocus their senior adult ministry efforts.

This chapter and the next will discuss basic and advanced issues pertaining to the organization and functioning of an effective senior adult ministry. All of the information is based on the responses received from more than 1,000 congregations from across the country.

Organization

In my first study, I asked 754 pulpit ministers the following question: "Do you have an organized senior adult ministry?" Twenty-five percent said "yes." The remaining respondents indicated "no" but several included a brief note stating, "We don't have a formal ministry for senior adults. We just take care of each other as the need arises." Interestingly, the size of the congregation was strongly related to the presence or absence of an organized senior adult ministry. Smaller congregations were much more likely to rely on informal senior adult ministry due, in large part, to limited finances and personnel. Larger congregations, on the other hand, typically had larger budgets and a greater number of ministers on staff which allowed for more specialized forms of ministry including senior adult ministry.

Informal ministry with senior adults can be very effective especially in smaller congregations. With fewer members, it is possible to be aware of individual needs and to quickly mobilize available resources in response to them. As the size of a church increases, though, there are an increasing number of hurdles to overcome in order to effectively use the talents of senior adult members while efficiently responding to needs within the congregation. As a result, a very important question about senior adult ministry involves the manner in which the ministry should be organized.

Ideally, every congregation could dedicate a full-time staff member to ministry with senior adults. My research indicates, however, that this is quite rare. Only 5% of senior adult ministries are directed by a full-time staff member. Approximately one in ten have a part-time senior adult minister. A more common arrangement is for the senior adult ministry to be placed under the general guidance of an elder or deacon. In some cases the senior adult

Figure 1
Senior Adult Minister on Staff?

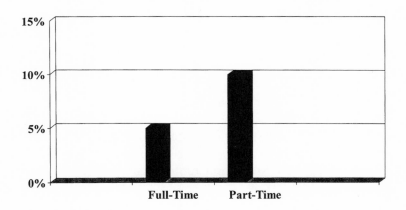

ministry is woven into the involvement ministry or the small group ministry.

A new method for organizing a senior adult ministry is beginning to appear. In an effort to create a ministry that is driven primarily by the senior adults, several congregations have formed a senior adult committee that oversees the activities of the group. The committee includes a chairperson and elected officers, one of which is typically an elder or deacon. The primarily role of the committee is to plan the activities of the senior adults and to mobilize them for service activities. Congregations in Alabama, Indiana, Kentucky, Mississippi, Texas, and Washington are utilizing this approach.

The Booneville, Mississippi Church of Christ has developed an extensive organizational structure. One individual serves as the "point person" for the senior adults

Figure 2
Organizational Structure of a Senior Adult Ministry

"Point Person"

"Steering Committee"

"Standing Committees"

Members of the Senior Adult Group

and the liaison with the elders and deacons. A core group of four to five individuals serves primarily as a steering committee. Several standing committees exist in order to respond to on-going needs among the senior adults and the congregation as whole. Finally, all of the senior adult members within the congregation are invited to be an active part of the group.

This method of organizing the senior adult ministry has been very effective because it is led entirely by volunteers. Although the Booneville congregation has a part-time senior adult minister on staff, he serves primarily in an advisory capacity. As a result, the senior adults are more invested in their program and adopt a philosophy of serving rather than being served.

Budget

One of the difficult tasks church leaders face is determining which ministry efforts will receive funding. The good news about senior adult ministry, in this regard, is that it can be a very inexpensive program. My research indicates that among churches with an organized senior adult ministry, 59% operate on less than $500 per year.

There are several reasons why it is possible to operate a senior adult ministry with such a small budget. First, the majority of senior adults have some form of income. If asked to use a small portion of that income to offset the expense that accompanies a project undertaken by the group, most are willing to do so. Second, the social and recreational expectations of senior adults tend to be more financially modest than those of other groups in the

Figure 3
Annual Budget for
Senior Adult Ministry

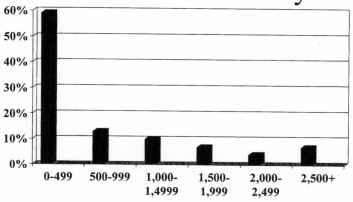

church. A weekly devotional followed by a social hour with coffee and donuts, a monthly potluck dinner or outing to a local restaurant, and an occasional overnight trip to a point of interest are among the more popular social events included in senior adult ministries today. Third, the vast majority of senior adult ministries today are not staff-driven. As a result, the costs associated with paying a full-time salary and benefits are avoided. The funds designated for senior adult ministry can go directly to the activities of the group.

A limited number of senior adult ministries have significantly larger budgets. As would be expected, these programs can afford to be far more creative and comprehensive due to the additional resources available to them. The higher allocation of dollars is usually found in larger congregations due to the size of the weekly contribution. In a few cases, however, the senior adult ministry has a benefactor. Some individuals choose to make a supplemental contribution to their congregation with the stipulation that the funds be used for ministry with senior adults. Others designate that a portion of their estate is to be given to the church in order to establish or expand the senior adult ministry. These funds are placed in an endowment with the proceeds being used to support the establishment or expansion of a senior adult ministry.

Involvement

Even the most well-organized, generously funded senior adult ministry will have a short life span unless additional members are added to the group. However, senior adult ministry is often seen as something designed

Figure 4
Issues in Recruitment
and Involvement

- Don't expect 100% participation
- Conduct a survey
- Involve the shut-ins
- Develop multiple groups

exclusively for "the old folks." Some of the image prob-lem can be traced to the underlying presence of disen-gagement theory in many senior adult ministries. A care-ful examination of the group's activities may reveal that a sizeable portion of their program consists of playing dominoes and taking a day trip to see wildflowers. As enjoyable as these activities may be to some, it is unlike-ly that they will appeal to everyone who could partici-pate in the senior adult ministry.

In response to the challenges of recruitment and involvement, leaders of a new or existing senior adult min-istry should keep several things in mind. First, don't expect 100% participation. Regardless of the age group, some members of the congregation do not want to participate in any activities other than the worship assemblies. While these individuals should continue to be invited to all group activities, their decision not to participate should be respected.

Second, conduct a survey of your senior adults. It is extremely difficult for one or two individuals to know what an entire group is capable of doing. By asking each person for their input, the program can accurately reflect the interests and talents of the senior adults in the congregation which can increase the level of participation. Additional surveys should be conducted periodically in order to stay abreast of changes within the group.

Third, identify ways to involve senior adult members who are shut-ins. The adage, "out of sight, out of mind," can quickly characterize a congregation's response to their shut-ins unless a concerted effort is made to include them in the activities of the church. Many shut-ins are physically limited but spiritually strong and are able to serve in marvelous ways if provided with an opportunity to do so. Prayer chains, telephone reassurance efforts, and correspondence with missionaries abroad are but a few of the innovative ways that shut-ins can be involved in meaningful ministry to others.

Finally, consider developing multiple senior adult groups. Older individuals are not homogeneous. They represent a diverse group educationally, financially, psychologically, socially, and spiritually. Developing subgroups within the senior adult ministry that are geared toward particular interests, abilities, or needs is an effective way to engage a larger number of senior adults in the program. Congregations in California, Mississippi, Tennessee, and Texas are using this approach and finding that it helps to extend the senior adult ministry to members who otherwise would not participate.

Names

Selecting a name for the senior adult ministry may seem relatively insignificant. However, the name of the group sets the tone for its activities and sends a message about its intended mission. Among the more popular names are "39ers," "Primetimers," "Senior Saints," and "Young at Heart." Other groups have adopted names that are more action-oriented. The names suggest that, rather than disengaging in their later years, senior adults can remain active and involved in social and spiritual growth, as well as meaningful service to others.

An example of an action-oriented name is the "Live Wires" at the Riverchase Church in Birmingham, Alabama. The leaders of the group describe the purpose of the "Live Wires" as being "to serve in any way possible, and to provide fellowship activities. Even though this is a senior/retiree group, we want to be active in doing the Lord's work as long as we are able, and we believe doing this together will bring us closer to each other, and also serve as an outreach to the community whenever opportunities arise."

At the Adams Boulevard Church in Bartlesville, Oklahoma, the name of the senior adult ministry is "Not Finished Yet." The name was selected because the leaders want "a distinct title and one that describes the spirit we see in some and that we want to instill in all – that of pressing on, never quitting. We may be 60, 70, 80, or 90, but there is still something we can do; we're not finished yet." The spirit of the "Not Finished Yet" group can also be seen in its objectives for the senior adult ministry:

1) To encourage all not to retire from life and service to God
2) To provide an opportunity to get to know each other and for fellowship
3) To provide an opportunity to be involved in service projects
4) To reach out to non-members by bringing friends and welcoming those who come
5) To provide educational and entertaining programs

In summary, establishing or expanding a senior adult ministry involves several issues. The manner in which the group will be organized, the level of funding available from the church, the approach to recruiting and involving senior adults, and the selection of an action-oriented name are key considerations to creating an environment in which a senior adult ministry can flourish. Once these matters are resolved, attention can then be focused on the more advanced issues of senior adult ministry.

Four

Programs in Senior Adult Ministry

Having addressed basic operational issues in senior adult ministry, we now turn our attention to programming. Across the country a number of creative programs exist. At the same time, a common core of programs can also be found. We will begin this chapter by examining the programs that are seen most frequently in senior adult ministry. Following that, we will consider the more innovative efforts using the "3 S's" (social, service, and spiritual) as our framework.

Core Programs

Among congregations with an organized senior adult ministry, a handful of programs are seen quite frequently. Visiting shut-ins is an extremely popular and important component of a senior adult ministry. Though the health status of senior adults today is better than ever before, many individuals do face the challenge of health difficulties on a regular basis. In some cases chronic illnesses

Figure 1
Popular Programs

- Visit Shut-ins
- Transportation to Church
- Christmas Basket
- Cassette Tape of Sermon
- Communion in Home
- Transportation to Shop
- Handyman Service
- Telephone Reassurance

---

create a situation in which people are unable to leave their home at all. Providing a regular visit to these individuals and keeping them abreast of congregational news will be greatly appreciated and can be vitally important to their well-being.

Providing an environment that makes the church building accessible to people with limited mobility is another important component of a senior adult ministry. Eliminating the physical barriers that could keep a senior adult from participating in the worship service is important because it communicates to the entire congregation that everyone is welcomed in the assembly. The external aspects of accessibility include providing transportation to worship services, designating reserved parking, and designing entrances to the building that do not require climbing steps. Once inside, reserved seating, hearing assistance devices, and large print Bibles and songbooks will allow every member of the congregation to participate in the worship service.

Including the core programs in a senior adult ministry is important because it provides the opportunity for every member of the congregation, regardless of age or health limitations, to participate in the worship assembly. However, if the senior adult ministry consists exclusively of the core programs, then the old model of ministry TO senior adults is clearly in place. A church which embraces the new model of ministry WITH senior adults will include the core programs but will also provide ample opportunities for social, service, and spiritual growth.

Social

Within the framework of the "3 S's," the "social" component seems to receive the greatest amount of attention. A quick overview of most senior adult ministries reveals that the calendar of events is full of social activities. To an outside observer the abundance of social events is often interpreted as an indication that senior adults simply like to "play." However, the importance of social interaction in the later stages of life is extremely important. One of the challenges that accompanies later life is the risk of social isolation. Retirement, widowhood, or a major change in living arrangements or health status can all lead a person to gradually enter into a state of isolation. Researchers have found, however, that the presence of a strong social support network can help an individual to deal more effectively with the challenges that may

Figure 2
The 3 "S's"

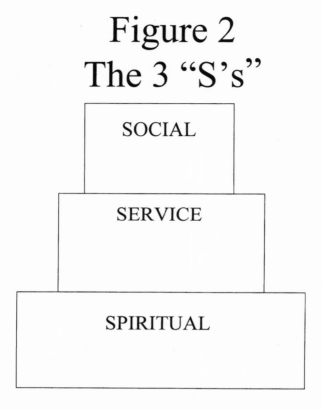

accompany the later years.[1] As a result an important part of the new model of senior adult ministry is the development of opportunities for social interaction.

Although a variety of social activities are available, most of them can be grouped into one of two categories. The first classification includes regularly scheduled events such as potluck dinners. Quarterly, monthly, or even bi-weekly fellowship meals are an extremely popular social activity among senior adult groups. The gatherings usually include more than just a meal, however. As a part of the fellowship time, other important activities can take place, including planning for future events, sharing information about needs within the group or the congregation, listening to a guest speaker, or simply enjoying an entertaining presentation.

Another regularly scheduled activity that includes a strong social element is the production of a senior adult newsletter. Not everyone will be able to attend the fellowship meals due to scheduling conflicts or health limitations. Distributing a monthly publication will allow every senior adult member, including the shut-ins, to stay abreast of news and events that impact them. The newsletter can include reports on previous activities, updates on issues pertinent to the group, editorials, photographs, humorous pieces, and even a crossword puzzle.

The second main classification of social activities includes the periodic trips that occur throughout the year. Many senior adult groups include day trips or overnight excursions in their repertoire of activities. The day trips are usually modestly priced outings to a place or event within a couple of hours of the church building. Visiting museums or theaters, attending a ballgame, or organizing a picnic at a state park are but a few of the many possibilities. In some cases an overnight stay is required due to the distance that must be traveled to the site or the amount of time that is needed to fully enjoy the activity or event. Examples of overnight trips can include seeing the blooming of the wildflowers in the spring or the changing of the leaves during autumn, traveling to the beach, or taking a trip on a cruise ship.

In planning social activities, two things should be kept in mind. First, the senior adult members may have a wide range of financial ability to pay for social activities. Thus, every effort should be made to keep the group-sponsored events at a reasonable level. This can occur by selecting modestly priced outings or having funds available to offset the cost of travel. If the latter option is selected, then the cost of everyone's trip should be reduced rather than offering scholarships for those who are in need. Individuals with limited financial resources may shy away from participating in the events if it requires that they "borrow" money from someone in order to attend. Reducing the cost of the trip can occur by using some of the budgeted funds for senior adults or privately accepting supplemental donations from members of the group.

A second consideration that a senior adult ministry may have to face is finding a person who is able and willing to drive the church bus or van. Many insurance companies do not allow "older" drivers to operate the vehicles owned by the local congregation. As a result the senior adults must find someone who is interested in their activities, available to drive the bus or van when the trip is scheduled, and "chronologically eligible" to operate the vehicle. An effective response to this challenge is to continue recruiting younger senior adults who are eligible to operate the church vehicles or identifying members of the congregation who are willing to serve as ongoing drivers for the senior adult trips.

Service
Social activities are a great way to begin a senior adult ministry and to keep people involved. However, if the

senior adult ministry is characterized entirely by social events and activities, then the old model of senior adult ministry remains in place. Increasingly, congregations around the country are moving beyond the purely social aspects of senior adult ministry and are developing ways to fully utilize the talents of their senior adult members. One of the key functions of the senior adult ministry is helping to match senior adults who want to serve with individuals or projects that need assistance. Although the possibilities are numerous, many of these opportunities fall into one of three general categories.

First, senior adults can serve other senior adults. Within the new model of ministry WITH senior adults, there will always be people who need to be ministered TO on a temporary or on-going basis. The senior adults in a congregation can be a wonderful source of encouragement and support during difficult times due to the wisdom and experience they have gained through the challenges of life. Senior adults can serve other senior adults in nursing homes, hospitals, or personal residences. The service can include fairly simple tasks like a regularly scheduled phone call to check on the individual's well-being, an occasional note of encouragement, or a personal visit during a particularly difficult time. Other service opportunities will require a greater commitment of time but will be just as meaningful. Assisting with transportation needs, sitting with a family at the hospital during an operation or extended illness, or providing lawn maintenance and minor home repairs will also help to meet the needs of senior adult members of the congregation.

Second, senior adults can also serve the entire congregation. In many churches senior adult members fold the bulletin, keep the pews supplied with attendance cards and sharpened pencils, and prepare the trays for communion. Senior adults are also actively involved in teaching Bible classes, organizing Vacation Bible Schools, and serving as elders and deacons. In a growing number of churches, the senior adult ministry is spearheading efforts to create intergenerational ties between the various age groups in the congregation. Popular programs such as "adopting a grandparent" and hosting a sweetheart banquet for the primetimers are being reversed as senior adults "adopt a teenager" or serve as surrogate grandparents to young families. At a time when many families are characterized by both parents working full-time jobs, the time and wisdom that a senior adult individual or couple can offer to the family often proves to be invaluable.

Finally, senior adults can serve the larger community. As they participate in various service projects, senior adults frequently become ambassadors for the Lord. As individuals or in a group, senior adults are making significant contributions to improving the quality of life for children by working tirelessly in after school programs, children's homes, and pediatric wards of hospitals. Working shoulder to shoulder with much younger people, senior adults are helping economically disadvantaged families to have a safe and decent place to live through the Habitat for Humanity program. Senior adults can also be found volunteering their time for the benefit of elderly individuals in the community by working with social service agencies in programs such as Meals on Wheels.

The opportunities for service are limitless but they must reflect the interests and abilities of the individuals who comprise the senior adult ministry. Opportunities to serve other senior adults, members of the entire congregation, or the community at large should be posted on a bulletin board and announced to the senior adults during their social gatherings. Every effort should be made to include as many different people as possible in the various service projects in order to create a larger base of volunteers and to avoid "burn out" by constantly calling on the same individuals to serve.

Spiritual

Social events and service projects may abound but without a strong spiritual emphasis the senior adult ministry will not serve its ultimate purpose. As is the case with all believers, senior adults need the opportunity to nourish their faith and grow in their knowledge of the Lord. As a result the spiritual component of the 3 "S's" is the foundation upon which the other elements are based.

In the majority of senior adult ministries, a time for Bible study and prayer beyond the regularly scheduled Sunday and Wednesday gatherings is available. Typically, these devotional times occur on a Tuesday or Thursday morning once or twice a month. The program usually consists of songs, prayers, and a devotional thought based on a selected passage of Scripture. Though guest speakers are invited from time to time, the program is usually organized and delivered by a member of the senior adult group.

In some congregations two Wednesday evening services are offered. One is at the usual evening hour but the other is scheduled for early in the afternoon. The earlier service is designed primarily for those who do not want to drive at night. By offering the alternative time, individuals are able to participate in the mid-week worship without having to compromise their decision to avoid night driving.

In addition to the more frequently seen options, a number of innovative opportunities for spiritual growth are beginning to emerge. Church camp for seniors, "golden agers" rallies, and teams of senior adult missionaries are flourishing in various parts of the country. Wonderful examples of spiritual renewal and effective evangelism are occurring in these settings. An increasing number of innovative programs will continue to appear as additional congregations adopt the new model of ministry WITH senior adults.

Conclusion

In summary, a careful examination of the 3 "S's" reveals that, rather than being mutually exclusive, the programs frequently overlap. Events that are designed primarily for service frequently include social elements within them. Periods of Bible study and prayer often conclude with a time for fellowship and socializing. Even social activities can provide a sense of spiritual renewal due to the encouragement that comes from being with fellow believers. As a result it is important to emphasize that the 3 "S's" must be seen as a framework for senior adult ministry rather than a checklist of "do's" and "do nots." Congregations with well-developed senior adult ministries seek to blend social, service, and spiritual elements without overdoing one at the expense of another. In chapter 5 we will examine several innovative programs that are providing social, service, and spiritual opportunities in their efforts to minister WITH senior adults.

Five

Exemplary Senior Adult Ministries

I n Chapter 3 I noted that 25% of the respondents to my first survey said that their congregation had an organized senior adult ministry. While this is encouraging news, the degree to which the 3 "S's" are seen in these programs varies considerably. Quite often the "social" aspect of senior adult ministry is far more prevalent than the "service" or "spiritual" elements, though the latter "S's" are beginning to appear more frequently. In a few cases, however, exemplary senior adult ministries are in place and provide excellent examples of how to effectively blend the 3 "S's."

In this chapter we will briefly examine eight senior adult ministries that are truly innovative. Selecting eight was not an easy task. An increasing number of congregations across the country are embracing the new model and developing effective ways of ministering WITH senior adults (Figure 1). The eight programs that are included have been chosen because they are among the best examples of what ministry with senior adults can encompass for those who are willing to adopt the new model.

Figure 1
Outstanding Senior Adult Ministries

- Searcy, Arkansas
- Crestwood, Kentucky
- Springfield, Missouri
- Belpre, Ohio
- Bartlesville, Oklahoma
- Georgetown, Texas
- Gainesville, Florida

Booneville, Mississippi

Name of Congregation: Booneville Church of Christ
Worship Attendance: 450-500
Members Age 65+: 25%
Group Name: The Golden Circle
Senior Adult Minister: Part-Time (J. A. Thornton)

"We call ourselves the Golden Circle because we are in our golden years and a circle never ends," explains part-time senior adult minister J. A. Thornton. Using the organizational framework identified in Chapter 4, members of the "Golden Circle" actively participate in numerous social, service, and spiritual activities.

On the first Tuesday of every month, the "Golden

Circle" gathers for a potluck meal and a time of fellowship. Each month a different individual or couple accepts responsibility for organizing the food preparation and the program that follows the meal. Informative speakers, entertaining presentations, and topics for group discussion are a few of the program alternatives. Although the monthly gathering is intended for the "Golden Circle," any members of the congregation are welcome to attend. In addition the "Golden Circle" fellowship meal provides an opportunity to reach out to seniors in the community in an evangelistic effort.

Members of the "Golden Circle" are also actively involved in service projects within their group and the congregation as a whole. The senior adults conduct a monthly devotional at the local nursing home, assist with refreshments during Vacation Bible School, and are key contributors to the congregation's "Helping Hands" ministry. Through an intergenerational effort that involves the entire congregation, "Helping Hands" provides assistance with minor carpentry and electrical work, house cleaning, transportation, yard work, and health needs. Some members of the "Golden Circle" also participate in the "traveling mission team." Rather than using their recreational vehicles for pleasure only, the group travels to U.S. mission fields and assists with door-to-door campaigns and Vacation Bible Schools.

Bandera, Texas

Name of Program: Golden Agers Camp
Number in Attendance: 125
Camp Director: Buck Griffith

Sponsoring Congregation: Windsor Park Church of Christ
Corpus Christi, Texas

Every September they gather in the hill country of
Texas for a week of fun, fellowship, and spiritual renewal. Like most Christian camps, they sleep in cabins, eat in
a mess hall, and prepare skits for the closing night talent
show. But there is something very different about this
group. Unlike the typical group of campers, these individuals range in age from their mid 50s to their mid 90s.
Under the direction of the Windsor Park Church of Christ,
the "Golden Agers Camp" just completed its 21st year.
"We started in 1981 with 35 campers," says camp director
Buck Griffith, "but now we average 125-130 each year."
The camp begins on Thursday evening and concludes on
the following Tuesday morning. The schedule of activities
is very similar to any church camp, though a few accom-
modations are necessary. The campers like to take field
trips, play games, sing, and just have a good time inter-
acting with one another.

The highlight of the week is the Monday night talent
show where campers display their musical, theatrical,
and comical abilities. In an evening filled with laughter
and applause, the "Golden Agers" entertain one another
and announce the recipients of the "Outstanding Male
and Female Camper" awards.

Since the purpose of the camp includes spiritual
growth as well as social interaction, a theme is chosen
each year that serves as the basis for all of the Bible study
and devotional activities. Several periods of singing,
praying, and study of Scripture are included in the daily

schedule, including the evening gathering at a nearby church building that members of the surrounding community are invited to attend. All of the teachers and guest speakers are campers who volunteer their time and energy in order to make the week's activities affordable to everyone and spiritually renewing.

Marysville, Ohio

Name of Congregation: St. John's Lutheran Church/St. Paul's Lutheran Church
Worship Attendance: 540
Members Age 65+: 14%
Group Name: Golden Eagles and Silver Eagles
Senior Adult Minister: None

"We like to crash churches!" jokes Herb Mock as he describes the process in which the "Golden Eagles" travel to other churches and join in their worship assembly. "You should see the looks on people's faces," he continues, "when a bus pulls up in front of their church and out piles 70 senior adults! It's a lot of fun."

Having fun and encouraging one another are the hallmarks of the "Golden Eagles" and their younger counterparts the "Silver Eagles." However, the scope of their activity extends well beyond social events. When the leaders of St. John's and St. Paul's Lutheran Churches decided to jointly form a senior adult ministry, they did so with a goal of encouraging senior adults to remain active in the life of the church. Despite their strong emphasis on this objective, most of their early efforts involved ministry to senior adults with numerous trips and social events being scheduled. Gradually the focus of the group began to shift toward ministry with, and by, senior adults rather than just ministry to them.

Nowhere is this change more apparent than in the Spiritual Mentoring Program in which members of the "Golden Eagles" and "Silver Eagles" adopt children from the St. John's School. The mentoring program involves linking a senior adult member of the church with one of the children from the congregation who is attending the school. The mentor receives a picture of the child, as well as a reminder of the commitment they are making. The mentor agrees to pray for the child daily and to be involved in his or her life on a regular basis. Though the program is meant primarily to focus on spiritual mentoring, in many cases it evolves into far more. Because the mentor and the child stay together from one school year to the next, the relationship is able to grow and frequently develops into a long-term friendship that is mutually beneficial.

Dallas, Texas

Name of Congregation: Skillman Church of Christ
Worship Attendance: 550
Members Age 65+: 40%
Group Name: Senior Adult Ministry & Sandwich
        Generation
Senior Adult Minister: Full-Time (Dr. Jim Hughes)

The senior adult ministry at the Skillman Church of Christ consists of nearly 40 different ministries. In addition to the core programs identified in the previous chapter, three of the programs are extremely innovative.

First, several of the senior adult members volunteer within the community. Some work with elementary school children in an after-school program. Senior adults travel to the neighborhood school and assist students who need additional instruction and practice in reading, math, and other subject areas. Several senior adults are also actively involved in working with aging agencies primarily for the benefit of other senior adults at the Skillman congregation.

The second innovative program deals with housing for senior adults. In an effort to provide living arrangements tailored to the changing needs of their senior adult members, several churches have proposed building an assisted living facility or nursing home. The leaders at Skillman have responded to this portion of their senior adult ministry in an unusual way. Rather than building their own retirement housing complex, they have negotiated a "group plan" with a local retirement housing company. An entire floor of one of the buildings in the retirement complex has been reserved for members of the Skillman congregation who are interested in moving. The initial fees are lower and the annual increases are capped for individuals living on this floor. Dr. Hughes is able to serve as an advocate to the management on behalf of those who have ties to the Skillman church. He is also permitted to conduct regular Bible studies within the facility.

Finally, the Skillman Church of Christ has recently begun a new senior adult ministry. Dr. Hughes recognized a challenge that occurs in many congregations. The members of his senior adult group were "aging in place" and very few younger individuals were participating in the group's activities. In response, he began the "sandwich generation" group which is designed primarily for individuals in their 50's and 60's who are raising their children AND caring for an older family member. The group meets monthly for a support group luncheon and shares their caregiving challenges from the previous month. Each person's caregiving experience serves as a case study that will eventually be used to develop a handbook for those who are faced with caregiving responsibilities on both ends of the family life cycle. Not only does the "sandwich generation" group provide support for those currently involved in caregiving relationships, it also serves as a bridge by which younger adults are able to gradually enter the larger work of the senior adult ministry.

Tuscaloosa, Alabama

Name of Congregation: University Church of Christ
Worship Attendance: 554
Members Age 65+: 12%
Group Name: Grand Adults
Senior Adult Minister: None

An interesting thing happened to the senior adult women at the University Church of Christ. A few years ago, several young ladies within the congregation asked the "Grand Adults" to serve as mentors to them during their collegiate experience at the University of Alabama. Eager to help, the "Grand Adults" women quickly mobilized and established a mentoring network with the college co-eds. The program has been mutually beneficial to the college students and the senior adult women and represents a wonderful intergenerational program that matches the enthusiasm of youth with the wisdom of age.

The "Grand Adults" also participate in several other social, service, and spiritual activities. The group has regularly scheduled game nights and travels to a nearby city for dinner once each quarter. The senior adult men are actively involved in transporting food from various community service agencies to the church building where it is packed into boxes and distributed to families in need. The local prison ministry was started by a man from the "Grand Adults" and is now an active intergenerational program within the University Church of Christ. The men are also in charge of folding and distributing the church bulletin.

The senior adult women make "love bears" that are given to children in local hospitals. The "love bears" are also distributed to the woman's shelter and the police department so that children from dysfunctional families can have a toy to call their own. The "love bear" project has been so successful that recently one social service agency contacted the "Grand Adults" and asked for 3,000 bears for their location.

Members of the "Grand Adults" actively participate in "Anna's Army," a prayer group consisting of women of various ages within the church. Using the monthly newsletter produced by the "Grand Adults," each member of the group prays for every person and need identified in the publication. "Anna's Army" makes a deliberate effort to include homebound individuals in their efforts. Rather than simply praying for them, the homebound women are encouraged to participate with the group and pray on behalf of other individuals. This is a marvelous way to include people in meaningful ministry even though their physical limitations do not allow them to travel from their home.

Gainesville, Florida
Name of Congregation: Westside Baptist Church
Worship Attendance: 1,200
Members Age 65+: 22%
Group Name: Saints Alive
Senior Adult Minister: Part-Time (Tom LaMee)

The senior adult ministry at the Westside Baptist Church is guided by the 24 member "Saints Alive Ministry Council." Consisting of representatives from each of the senior adult Bible classes, directors of special care ministries, and a member of the church's full-time ministry staff, the Ministry Council plans a variety of social, service, and spiritual activities for the senior adult Christians.

With the exception of the summer months, the "Saints Alive" meet on the first Thursday of the month for a time of fellowship and devotion. During their meeting they eat together, share news that is pertinent to the group, have a period of Bible study and prayer, and usually listen to a guest speaker. Prior to the entire group gathering, the Ministry Council meets to discuss current business and upcoming events. On the third Thursday of each month, the "Saints Alive" have an "away event." This usually consists of a day trip to a point of interest within driving distance that typically includes sight seeing, shopping, or dining out. Occasionally the trip will include an overnight stay.

In addition to their regularly scheduled monthly activities, the "Saints Alive" have two primary outreach events each year. These events are intended not only to encourage members of the group but also to reach out to senior adults in the community. In December the senior adults and the church staff gather for a Lord's Supper service in which they celebrate the resurrection of Christ by partaking of the Lord's Supper. Following their time of worship, they enjoy a Christmas banquet together. In May the "Saints Alive" enjoy a country picnic that they call a "Corn Boil." Using only items that are fresh from the garden, the senior adults travel to the farm of one of their members and enjoy a day of food and fellowship.

Every other year the "Saints Alive" undertake an ambitious project when they host an area-wide senior adult conference. Beginning at 8:30 with registration and concluding by mid-afternoon, the conference consists of keynote addresses, several breakout sessions, periods of worship, and a catered lunch with decorations. The conference has met with great success attracting more than 100 senior adults from the Westside Church as well as churches from the surrounding counties.

Lubbock, Texas

Name of Program: Senior Adventures in Ministry
*Number of Participants: 60
*Director: Stuart Jones
*Sponsoring Congregation: Sunset Church of Christ

"Senior Adventures in Ministry" (SAIM) is one of the newest units in the Sunset International Bible Institute.

Since its inception in January of 1995, more than 60 senior adults have been prepared for ministry roles in the United States and abroad. A primary objective of the SAIM program is to help senior adults identify their unique gifts and determine how to use them in service to the Lord by serving others. Since many of the students enter the program following an episode of loss in their life, support groups are quickly established to provide assistance to individuals as they move through the grieving process. The bonds that are established allow for a strong team orientation to develop as individuals with varied backgrounds come together with the common purpose of preparing for ministry.

Though every student completes a basic course in ministry, the SAIM curriculum is meant to be flexible and has a strong practical orientation. Students are permitted to enroll in credit bearing courses that are offered within the broader curriculum of the Sunset International Bible Institute but are not required to do so.

During their time in Lubbock, SAIM students attend chapel and are introduced to ministry opportunities within the United States and in foreign countries. Students are encouraged to participate in the annual campaigns that alternate between a stateside and overseas location. The combination of classroom instruction, chapel presentations, and direct experience in a mission field assists the SAIM students in determining how and where they can serve most effectively in the Lord's Kingdom. Although some SAIM students may become full-time pulpit ministers, the vast majority choose to serve in other equally meaningful roles.

Murfreesboro, Tennessee

Name of Congregation: North Boulevard Church of Christ
Worship Attendance: 1,386
Members Age 65+: 10%
Group Name: Young at Heart
Senior Adult Minister: Part-Time (Winston Schloot)

The North Boulevard Church of Christ sponsors one of the largest "Meals on Wheels" programs in Murfreesboro, Tennessee. Though the program is not officially a part of the "Young at Heart" ministry, it depends heavily on the volunteer efforts of the senior adult members in the congregation. "Young at Heart" members play a vital role in preparing, packaging, and delivering the meals that help sustain nearly 40 older members of the church, as well as many in the community. Three hot meals, along with two additional meals that can be heated by the recipient, are delivered on a weekly basis.

Participation in the Meals on Wheels program is but one of the many facets of the "Young at Heart" program. According to the group's mission statement, the "Young at Heart" ministry is designed to "encourage our senior citizens to be active in the ministries at North Boulevard, as well as to minister to those seniors who have spiritual or physical needs." "Young at Heart" members seek to accomplish this goal by organizing numerous service opportunities, including shopping for shut-ins, telephone reassurance, home repair, and auto maintenance. A major component of the group's ministry efforts involves visitation in local hospitals, nursing homes, and personal residences. Through periodic collections, members of the "Young at Heart" group fund and deliver "goody bags" to local hospitals. The bags contain snack foods, note pads, and half a roll of quarters that can be used to make phone calls or purchase drinks from vending machines. The "goody bags" are delivered to the family of any member of the North Boulevard congregation who is hospitalized.

As important as their service projects are, members of the "Young at Heart" group also participate in regularly scheduled social activities. In addition to an occasional day or overnight trip, a "Young at Heart" luncheon is scheduled for every fourth Friday excluding November and December when special holiday gatherings are organized. The luncheons are designed to promote fellowship and encouragement, as well as to provide an opportunity to raise awareness of needs among members of the group.

Conclusion

The eight examples in this chapter were selected because they clearly illustrate the new model of senior adult ministry. Though different combinations of the "3 S's" are in place, the common denominator in the eight programs is the belief that Christians can remain actively involved in ministry even in their later years.

Six

"Pillars of Faith"

The new model of senior adult ministry is possible because individuals are living longer, healthier, and more active lives. In some cases, the increase in life expectancy is being used simply to indulge in hobbies and recreational activities. In other cases, however, the "golden years" are being used not only to pursue personal interests but also to engage in service to others. This chapter will introduce nine "pillars of faith" who have chosen to remain active servants of the Lord in their sixth, seventh, eighth or ninth decade of life.

Guy Yowell

Caring for the needs of individuals, both physically and spiritually, has been the distinguishing characteristic of Guy Yowell's ministry for more than half a century. As a church leader in Sherman, Texas, he has served as an elder, deacon, and Bible class teacher. But Guy's acts of kindness and service extend well beyond these highly visible roles. As one of the early adopters of a Christian filmstrip series, Guy presented the gospel to many individuals and played a part in a number of conversions, though he humbly says he can't remember how many.

While faithfully working as a personal evangelist, he also balanced his job and family responsibilities. Even when his wife's health reached the point where she needed constant care, Guy managed to lovingly provide for her while maintaining an active concern for others. During the period of grief that followed her death, Guy began accumulating resources on grief recovery to help him work through his loss. As his own grief gradually subsided, he began using his knowledge and experience to minister to others by becoming a hospice volunteer. For countless hours, Guy sat with terminally ill patients offering companionship and encouragement.

Having just celebrated his ninetieth birthday, Guy no longer drives his car which has lead to a restructuring of his ministry efforts. But far from disengaging, he has simply modified his grief recovery efforts by focusing primarily on individuals with whom he is already acquainted. He regularly provides access to his library of grief recovery materials, sends cards of encouragement, and offers reassurance to others via the telephone.

Chelsea Reed

If you are a member of the Churches of Christ in the mid-Ohio Valley, there is a strong possibility that your life has been touched by Chelsea Reed. "Brother Reed," as he is affectionately known, has been an active servant in the Lord's church for more than 70 years. During that time, he has served as an elder, preacher, Bible class teacher, song leader, and personal evangelist for several congregations including the 34th Street congregation in Vienna, West Virginia, and the North End congregation in Parkersburg, West Virginia.

Even though he has frequently held leadership positions, Brother Reed is best known for two things. First, until a medical condition in his throat forced him to stop, the pleasing sound of his high tenor singing voice was easily discernable in every worship service or gospel sing he attended. Second, and perhaps more importantly, Brother Reed's tireless visitation efforts in local hospitals and nursing homes are well known. While still a young man, he developed the habit of not eating lunch. Instead, he used the time to visit in the local hospitals. This act of service continued even when Brother Reed was forced to retire from full-time employment due to his age. In addition to caring for his wife, Gaynelle, until her death in 1989, Brother Reed maintained his active visitation efforts.

Today, at the age of 92, he pays a brief visit to every hospitalized individual in Parkersburg, West Virginia, who lists "Churches of Christ" as their religious affiliation in the hospital registry. Even as the arthritis in his knees has worsened, his visitation work has not diminished. In fact, with the completion of the Churches of Christ-sponsored "Love and Care Nursing Home," Brother Reed has added another stop in his visitation work!

Ed Springer

If anyone deserves the title of "prayer warrior," it is Ed Springer. For more than seven decades, the 93 year old has been an active servant of the Lord, initially at the Baptist Tabernacle in Atlanta and more recently at the First Baptist Church in Smyrna, Georgia. Since becoming a Christian at the age of 21, he has been personally sharing the good news of Jesus and faithfully praying on behalf of himself and others.

Ed's perspective on communicating with God has been shaped by years of study and prayer. Through times of happiness and sorrow, he has maintained his belief that God answers prayer. The depth of his faith is perhaps best illustrated by his statement that "I use to think God wasn't answering my prayers when I would pray for someone who was sick and then they would die, but now I understand that God has taken them home to heal them."

Though his health and circle of friends has declined in recent years, Ed's faith remains strong because he continues to nourish it. According to senior adult minister, Doug Allen, Ed applies the adage of "use it or lose it" to both his physical and spiritual well-being. In addition to his daily walks inside the local shopping mall, during which he frequently shares his faith with fellow walkers, Ed regularly attends the worship assemblies of First Baptist Church, sings in the senior adult choir, and participates in two men's prayer groups. He participates in all these activities despite the fact that he doesn't drive anymore and has difficulty seeing. Undeterred, he calls on members of his family to help with his transportation needs and when the senior adult choir learns a new song, Ed compensates for his poor vision by listening to the song on a cassette tape until he has memorized the lyrics and the music.

Participating in the worship service, choir, and prayer groups are important to Ed, but they are also inspiring to those around him. His lifelong commitment to Christ and unswerving belief in the power of prayer provide encouragement to all who know him.

Dean Martin

Ninety-three-year-old Dean Martin can really work a crowd! His friendly personality and love of people are evident before and after every gathering of the Western Heights Church of Christ in Sherman, Texas. With a smile on his face and a pocket full of chewing gum for the children, Dean circulates through the auditorium greeting old friends and making new acquaintances.

Beneath his gregarious demeanor, Dean has a deep commitment to the Lord, as well as a keen interest in the legal system. During his formative years, Dean became a Christian and entered into a life of service to others that continues today. Frequently, he has used his knowledge of the law for benefit of the church and individuals within it.

A defining moment in Dean's life came while serving as the prosecuting attorney for Grayson County, Texas, during the 1960s. A defendant was charged with first degree murder and it was Dean's responsibility to uphold the law by seeking the death penalty. Though personally opposed to capital punishment, Dean successfully prosecuted the case and the defendant received the death penalty. Having fulfilled his professional obligation, Dean immediately took steps to ensure the man's eternal future. He contacted a minister and made arrangements for him to study the Bible with the condemned prisoner, which eventually lead to his conversion. When word of his efforts reached Grayson County, Dean was heavily criticized for being "soft" on crime. Despite the opposition, Dean remained emphatic that the man's eternal destiny was significantly more important than his physical one.

Following his years as an elected official, Dean returned to private practice and has remained active in his local congregation by serving as an elder, song leader, and occasional Bible class teacher. Though he recently closed his law office, he continues to practice law from his home. The vast majority of his work now involves assisting elderly individuals in the church, and the community at large, with the legal issues that accompany one's later years.

Ina Comeau

At the age of 62, Ina Comeau made an important decision. She decided it was time for a change. Although involved in church for years, Ina sensed a need to assume a new role in ministry. She was just not sure what that role should be. She approached her pastor, Phil Weaver, and sought guidance. The two began praying that God would show Ina the direction He intended for her to take.

While waiting for an answer to their prayers, Ina joined a ladies Bible study group. At the conclusion of one study session, a member of the group approached Ina and began telling her how much the residents in a local nursing home needed encouragement and enjoyed being visited. Ina heard in these words a new ministry opportunity. So she decided that she and her poodle, Blackie, would begin a visitation ministry. Their efforts were extremely well received and it appeared to Ina that she had found her new place of service.

After a year of developing her visitation program, Blackie died. Because Ina felt the key to the ministry was Blackie's presence, she thought her newfound efforts in serving others had ended. What she failed to realize, however, was that her perspective had changed. Not waiting for people to serve her, she had begun developing an increasing desire to serve others. During the time she had been visiting the nursing home, Ina had also become involved in teaching a ladies Sunday School class and completed a course on evangelism training. What appeared to be a setback in her ministry actually became a time to reflect on other avenues of service and considering how to continue her visits to the nursing home.

Today Ina serves in the ongoing ministries of the Friendship Baptist Church in Newark, Delaware, as a choir member, Sunday School teacher, and team leader in evangelistic outreach. Along with her husband, Pete, she continues to seek out new ways to become more effective in her ministry. She is also in the process of re-establishing her nursing home visitation with her new poodle, Rascal.

J. A. Thornton[1]

J. A. Thornton was born in a rural community in Mississippi in 1920. Weighing slightly more than two pounds, the prospects for his survival were not good. During the uncertainty of the days that immediately followed his birth, two important events occurred that would shape the future of the tiny baby. First, his mother prayed fervently for the baby's survival and promised the Lord that, if he lived, she would do all in her power to make him a gospel preacher. Second, an African-American woman came to the Thornton's home and assisted in the baby's care. Though it was August in the deep South, she insisted that a fire be started in the fireplace. She placed a rocking chair in front of the hearth and gently rocked the newborn all through the first day and night. Through the combination of prayer and attentive care, J. A. Thornton survived his fragile beginning.

As would be expected, his early days significantly shaped his direction in life. Not only did Thornton begin to share his mother's dream of a life committed to service in the Lord's church, he also developed a racial tolerance that was not widespread in the United States prior to the Civil Rights Movement. Following completion of his education at Freed-Hardeman College and Delta State Teachers College, Thornton taught school for one year while he served as a gospel preacher. His first full-time work with a congregation was in Ruleville, Mississippi. Since then he has worked with several congregations including his present ministry with the Booneville Church of Christ in Booneville, Mississippi, where he serves as the part-time senior adult minister. In a quiet and unpretentious manner, J. A. Thornton continues to fulfill the promise his mother made more than 80 years ago by preaching the gospel and gently ministering to the individuals around him.

John Henry Pruitt

John Henry Pruitt knows a thing or two about prison ministry. Since 1992 he has been actively involved with the prison ministry of the Windsor Park Church of Christ in Corpus Christi, Texas. The 74 year-old Pruitt regularly visits correctional facilities in south Texas and joyfully shares the good news of Jesus Christ. His message is a strong and convincing one because it includes his own story of conversion.

During his formative years in Fort Worth, Texas, John Henry began a career of petty theft and burglary that would eventually lead to his initial incarceration. In the years that followed, he was convicted of several subsequent offenses and served time in numerous state and federal correctional facilities. In fact, by the time he was released in 1992, John Henry Pruitt had spent 37 and a half years behind bars! But a transformation took place in 1986. While serving his final sentence in the Texas Department of Corrections, John Henry began to study the Bible with individuals from the Windsor Park congregation and was baptized into Christ. At the age of 59, John Henry Pruitt became a Christian and began a new way of life.

John Henry now lives in Corpus Christ and works part-time for the church and the city of Corpus Christi. His passion, however, is talking about the change that has occurred in his life and the freedom that he now experiences, both physically and spiritually.

Joe and MaryLou McKissick

Joe and MaryLou McKissick have a unique perspective on senior adult ministry. Following several years of local ministry within the United States and mission work in South Africa and Canada, the McKissicks moved to Abilene, Texas, in order to work in the Pruett Gerontology Center (PGC). For more than a decade, they have continued to minister to churches and individuals by combining their passionate interest in senior adult ministry with the lessons learned from two caregiving experiences.

In 1978 MaryLou's mother and father moved into the McKissick's home due to the deteriorating health of her father. During the progressive degeneration that accompanies Alzheimer's Disease, the McKissick's gently cared for her father until his death in 1984. Her mother continued to live with them until her death but gradually needed additional assistance due to macular degeneration[2] and eventually Parkinson's Disease. Though these times were challenging, the McKissick's patiently ministered to their family members and gained strength from each other. Based on their experiences, they are now able to speak candidly to audiences about the challenges of informal caregiving and the tremendous blessings that can come from it.

As significant as their caregiving experience is, the McKissick's involvement in the PGC stems most directly from Joe's vision for senior adult ministry that first began in the 1970s. While in Vancouver, Canada, Joe began to consider the changing role that senior adults would need to assume in order for local congregations to remain viable. He began to write articles and offer workshops on ministry with senior adults. When the McKissick's moved to Sugarland, Texas, he continued to emphasize the growing importance of senior adult ministry and began work on a graduate degree in gerontology through the PGC. Because of his pioneering work in this area, 75 year-old Joe McKissick remains a highly sought after speaker who travels nationally and internationally in order to educate church leaders and members about the growing importance of ministry with senior adults.

Conclusion

The nine individuals in this chapter are not "pillars of faith" because of an isolated incident. Rather, they are senior adult Christians who, in most cases, have been engaged in faithful service to the Lord for decades. Though their level of activity may have been modified as they have aged, their commitment to the work of the kingdom has remained strong.

While these individuals provide wonderful examples of senior adults who have remained engaged in ministry, the reality is that there are thousands of "pillars of faith" in churches across the country. Some are involved in very visible forms of ministry while others are engaged in ministry that tends to go unnoticed. In either case, they illustrate the tremendous capabilities that exist when churches choose to minister WITH, rather than just TO, senior adults.

Seven

Aging and the Human Body

Church leaders play an extremely important role in the lives of many senior adults. Research indicates that, beyond one's own family, senior adults are most likely to call on leaders of their church for assistance in times of need.[1] Unfortunately, the results of numerous studies also indicate that current and prospective ministers are poorly informed about the processes and realities of aging.[2] As a result, church leaders frequently find themselves in the difficult position of trying to minister to, and with, people about whom they know very little. It is vitally important, therefore, that elders, deacons, preachers, and any other person interested in ministry with senior adults develop a better understanding of the aging process.

This chapter and the next two are designed to provide a basic introduction to the biology, psychology, and sociology of aging for those who have not received formal training in this area. For those who are interested in learning more about a particular subject area, in-depth information is available by referring to the chapter notes located at the end of the book.

The Biology of Aging

In the opening chapter, the concept of life expectancy was identified as a major contributor to the aging of the population. In the twentieth century alone, approximately thirty years were added to life expectancy in the United States. Given the dramatic increase in a relatively short period of time, an optimistic view of the future would include the notion that human beings could live extremely long lives as advances in medical procedures and technology continue. It is generally accepted among researchers, however, that the human life span is limited to 120 years.[3] The combination of human genetics, personal habits, and the environment in which a person has lived greatly impacts life expectancy and the rate at which the human body ages.

While the process of aging is unique for every individual, some age-related changes are seen more commonly than others. In this chapter, we will examine the biology of the aging process by focusing on the skin, eyes, ears, skeleton, and heart.

Skin

The integumentary system consists of the skin, hair, nails, and various glands located in the skin. Its primary function is to maintain a stable internal environment for the body so that the vital organs can perform their roles.[4] Of all the changes that can take place in the human body, those that occur within the integumentary system are certainly the most noticeable. The loss of hair, or at least the changing color of it, along with the emergence of wrinkles, are a great concern for many individuals and provide the basis for a very lucrative cosmetic industry. Despite the best efforts of many to counter it, the reality is that the changing appearance of the integumentary system is a natural part of the aging process.

As we age our skin begins to lose the elasticity it had earlier in life. In addition, the layer of fat located deep within the structure of the skin begins to disappear. The net result is skin that wrinkles, sags, and does not snap back into place as quickly as it once did. While medical procedures, like face lifts and collagen implants, can temporarily restore the tautness of the skin, eventually the inevitable changes that accompany the aging process will reappear.

While the quest for youthful-looking skin is well publicized on television and in magazines, of far greater concern is the impact that changes in the skin can have on a bedfast person. Because the layer of fat that previously existed has gradually diminished, older individuals have less padding between their bones and skin. When left in the same sitting or lying position for extended periods of time, the pressure of the bone begins to wear away at the skin and produces a decubitus ulcer or "bedsore." Once a decubitus ulcer is established, it is extremely difficult to restore the integrity of the skin. Thus, it is far better to take the steps needed to avoid the initial appearance of a decubitus ulcer. Generally, these include turning the individual frequently and keeping the skin clean and dry.[5]

Vision

Of all the senses, the eyes are the first to show signs of aging.[6] As we age, the lens of the eye begins to thicken, develops a yellowish tint, loses its ability to focus on near objects or small print items, and eventually becomes cloudy. Most of these changes, however, are fairly common and can be dealt with effectively by prescription glasses or surgical procedures.

Presbyopia is an age-related condition of the eye that affects almost everyone after the age of 40.[7] With this condition, the ability of the eye to view near objects diminishes requiring the individual to hold the item farther away in order to be able to read it. In most cases, presbyopia is easily remedied by wearing bifocals or reading glasses.

Another fairly common age-related condition of the eye is cataracts, affecting nearly 90% of individuals over the age of 70.[8] A cataract is a lens that has become so clouded that it adversely affects an individual's ability to see. The condition of a cataract is similar to driving a car in a dense fog. The driver is able to distinguish images as they approach but it is difficult to see them clearly. Fortunately, cataracts can usually be quickly and safely removed in an outpatient surgery. The clouded lens is removed and an artificial lens is implanted or prescription glasses are worn.

In addition to the more common age-related changes in vision are several changes that are considered to be abnormal. Among those are macular degeneration and glaucoma. Though not limited exclusively to older individuals, macular degeneration is a disease affecting the retina that is more likely to occur in the later years of life. Persons with macular degeneration lose their central vision which makes it difficult to distinguish the fine details of items directly in front of the person. Unfortunately, surgical or medical procedures are rarely effective in treating macular degeneration although the use of magnifying glasses can help to overcome some of the loss of vision.[9]

Glaucoma is a disease that results from a buildup of pressure within the eye. Individuals who have glaucoma lose their peripheral vision and eventually develop tunnel vision. If left untreated, it can cause blindness. Unlike macular degeneration, however, glaucoma can be easily treated with eye drops, laser treatment, or surgery if it is detected early enough.[10]

Hearing

Presbycusis or the loss of hearing that is a normal part of the aging process typically begins to occur during the third decade of life due to changes in the inner ear structures. By the age of 50, an individual's ability to distinguish between the higher sound frequencies will typically have diminished to the point that it is noticeable and may begin to impact their daily interactions.[11]

While some form of hearing loss is present in approximately 80% of senior adults, most do not experience the complete loss of hearing.[12] For those who do, their condition is usually described as conductive deafness or nerve deafness. When the transmission of sound waves is blocked by something in the ear, then "conductive deafness" occurs. The blockage may be due to an inflammation of the eardrum, problems with the small vibrating bones in the ear, or simply an excessive accumulation of earwax. Since the inner part of the ear has not been damaged, responding to conductive deafness is relatively easy. Hearing loss caused by the buildup of earwax can be resolved by removing the blockage either with a visit to one's physician or by using an over-the-counter kit available in most pharmacies. If the hearing loss is due to a more permanent change in the structure of the ear then a hearing aid can be used to alter the condition.

In contrast to conductive deafness, "nerve deafness" is more serious because it results from adverse changes deep within the structure of the inner ear. Typically, hearing aids do not correct nerve deafness. However, cochlear implants can help an individual to restore the ability to hear, though the process rarely reproduces the same quality of sound that existed previously.

Skeletal System

Consisting of bone and cartilage, the skeletal system performs several important functions in the human body, including protection of the internal organs, formation of blood cells, providing a framework for the soft tissue, and serving as a point of attachment for muscles.[13] In addition, bones serve as an important storage location for several minerals, including calcium, that are needed by the body. Through a process known as "formation and resorption," bone is made and then broken down in order to release minerals needed by the body into the bloodstream. Until the age of 30, bone is formed at a faster rate than it is broken down which leads to a highly dense bone structure in most adolescents and young adults. After the age of 30, however, bone loss begins to occur as the rate of formation slows.[14]

Osteoporosis is the term used to describe bones that have become weakened when the rate of resorption exceeds the rate of formation. Although both men and women can experience osteoporosis, it is far more common among women and is thought to be related to the changes that are brought by the onset of menopause. It is estimated that half of all women over the age of 50 are affected by osteoporosis and that nearly all deal with it by the age of 70.[15] For the majority of people, the most noticeable result of osteoporosis is an increased likelihood of fracturing a bone which is why senior adults can be especially vulnerable to injury after a fall. In more advanced cases, a gradual loss of height occurs and the upper back or spine begins to curve which eventually leads to a condition known as "dowagers hump."

While osteoporosis deals with the structure of the bone, arthritis is a term used to describe the inflammation of joints. Technically, there are several forms of arthritis though the most common one is osteoarthritis. Affecting between 30 and 40 million Americans, osteoarthritis is the inflammation and eventual degeneration of the cartilage that covers the ends of bones.[16] Because this form of arthritis is so common among senior adults, it is often seen as being the result of the wear and tear that the body absorbs during one's lifetime. Regular, modest exercise that strengthens the joints and keeps them flexible is considered one of the best responses to osteoarthritis.[17]

Cardiovascular System

The cardiovascular system includes the heart, blood vessels, and blood. The primary function of the cardiovascular system is to supply oxygen and nutrients to the cells of the body and to remove the waste products from them.[18] When functioning properly, the heart pushes blood to the lungs where it receives oxygen and then returns to the heart. From there, the blood is pushed through a series of progressively smaller arteries to the various areas of the body. Through a system of veins, the blood returns to the heart and is then sent to the lungs for oxygen. This process continues, uninterrupted, as long as the cardiovascular system is functioning effectively.

As we age the cardiovascular system undergoes several changes including a loss of elasticity in the blood vessels. Normally, blood vessels are flexible and able to help move blood throughout the body. Blood vessels that become less pliable and clogged with waste material are characteristic of a condition known as arteriosclerosis or hardening of the arteries. When this occurs the heart has to work harder in order to distribute blood throughout the entire body. The extra strain placed on the heart can lead to hypertension or high blood pressure. Though hypertension is not limited to senior adults, it is more commonly seen among older individuals. The presence of hypertension for an extended period of time can contribute to heart attack, heart failure, kidney failure, or ruptured blood vessels.[19] The risk of hypertension can be reduced by eating a low sodium diet, exercising regularly, maintaining an appropriate body weight, and avoiding the use of tobacco products.

Implications for Ministry

The information in this chapter provides a baseline of knowledge about some of the biological changes that are part of the aging process. For people who intend to minister with senior adults, recognition of what constitutes "normal aging" is important especially in light of our youth-oriented culture and its efforts to deny the physical changes that are a natural part of moving through the life cycle. In addition to simply increasing one's knowledge of the aging process, this information has a number of practical implications as well.

First, since presbyopia is so common, consider increasing the font size in printed material such as songbooks, announcement sheets, and church bulletins. Even if it means changing the margins or adding some extra pages, remember your audience and design the written material accordingly. Also bear in mind that the lens of the eye develops a yellowish tint as we age. One of the important ramifications of this change is that it becomes increasingly more difficult to distinguish between colors on the blue/green end of the spectrum. Items intended for senior adults are far more likely to be noticed when they are printed on red or orange paper.

Second, be sensitive to the needs of the hearing impaired. One fairly common response is to make hearing assistance devices available for use during the worship service. Another step that can be taken includes selecting venues for group meetings that are relatively quiet. Large rooms such as restaurants, fellowship halls, and family life centers are often needed to accommodate the entire group but can be especially problematic for individuals with some degree of hearing loss because of the high level of background noise that is usually present. A simple response to this situation is to use the common areas when a large social event is being scheduled but to opt for the quiet and privacy of an office or personal residence when a more focused discussion is likely to occur.

Third, the high frequency of osteoporosis, arthritis, and hypertension among senior adults strongly suggests that providing information about these changes is a worthwhile component of a senior adult ministry. As a part of the social or service elements within the 3 S's, exercise classes and health fairs can be conducted on a regularly scheduled basis and local physicians can be invited to speak to the group about the latest medical news as it relates to these conditions as well as others that are of interest to senior adults. Programs such as these will not only be beneficial to the regular participants of the senior adult ministry but can also serve as an effective outreach to seniors within the church and the community at large.

Eight

The Aging Mind

Contrary to popular belief, most senior adults do not suffer from abnormal psychological conditions like Alzheimer's Disease. Instead, they experience a highly personalized journey through the life cycle that can include changes in learning, intelligence, personality, and attention. However, when considering the psychological changes that do accompany later life, the one that is of greatest interest to most people is memory loss. As a result, this chapter will focus on the various components of human memory and how they change during one's lifetime. We will also consider the different forms of dementia, including Alzheimer's Disease, in an effort to debunk some of the myths surrounding it.

Memory

In order to understand how memory works, we must first develop an understanding of the concept of attention. The world is full of many stimuli that we are able to notice using our sense of touch, taste, smell, vision, or hearing. Many of the stimuli, however, go unnoticed since we pay attention to a relatively small number of them. Once we have chosen the items that are of interest to us, an involved process of placing, storing, and retrieving the information in our memory system begins.

The part of memory where new information is first registered is referred to as "sensory memory." Information will only stay in the sensory memory for a few seconds.[1] If an individual does not pay attention to the information and move it into the next stage of memory then it simply disappears. "Working memory" is the part of the memory system where information can be retained for about 30 seconds.[2] Working memory is considered a crucial part of the entire memory system because so many different activities take place within it. Working memory is the where existing information can be held, combined with new information, and simultaneously used to solve a problem, learn something new, or make a decision.

"Long-term memory" is the location where information can be stored for a few seconds, a few minutes, or even several years.[3] Remembering an appointment, being able to follow a routine, or recalling directions to a particular destination are some of the many ways in which long-term memory is used every day. Finally, "remote memory," also known as "tertiary memory," is the part of the memory system where information can be held for extended periods of time.[4] Being able to recall the street address of one's childhood home or the name of an elementary school teacher from many years ago are some examples of the type of information that can be found in remote memory.

As important as placing information into the memory system is, retrieving the information is of equal importance. The results of many years of research indicate that the process of aging does impact certain parts of the memory system while not affecting others. For instance, sensory memory does not seem to be adversely affected by the aging process.[5] Though the ability to perceive stimuli may be altered due to changes in the five senses, the actual process of using sensory memory appears to remain unaffected. Similarly, remote memory does not seem to be altered by one's movement through the life cycle, though there has not been a great deal of research in this area.[6]

In contrast to sensory and remote memory, working and long-term memory are impacted by the aging process. As the mind ages the capacity of working memory appears to decline. Research indicates that older individuals can perform as well as younger individuals on tests of working memory when only one task is involved.[7] However, when asked to complete several tasks simultaneously, senior adults do not perform as well on the tests. It has been argued that the reason for the difference is found in the speed with which the information is processed. When tests of working memory are given and a time limit is not placed on completing multiple tasks, then the age-related differences virtually disappear.[8]

Long-term memory also appears to be impacted by the aging process. The findings of research studies indicate that senior adults have more difficulty accessing information in their long-term memory.[9] The process of retrieval is slower and less efficient for older people than for younger. In particular, senior adults have difficulty with tests of recall though they do well on tests of recognition. A recall test is one in which the individual is asked to remember some information given to them previously without the assistance of any hints or clues. One example of a test of recall is an essay exam in which a person is asked a question and required to retrieve the entire response from memory. A recognition test, on the other hand, is one in which the individual is provided with some assistance in completing the task. Multiple choice and true/false exams are both examples of tests of recognition. An encouraging finding from research studies is that senior adults can improve their long-term memory through training and practice.[10] Typically, older persons do not use study techniques that have been found to effectively improve long-term memory. When taught how to use them, senior adults are able to improve their performance on tests of long-term memory.

Dementia

Dementia is a generic term that is used to describe a group of mental disorders caused by microscopic changes in the brain. It affects memory, cognitive functions, and personality to such a degree that normal activity and social functioning are severely interrupted.[11] In addition to the reversible forms that are caused by anemia, depression, the interaction of medications, or poor diet, there are approximately twelve different types of non-reversible dementia.[12]

One form of dementia can occur following a stroke. Also known as a "cerebrovascular accident," a stroke occurs when blood vessels in the brain are blocked or ruptured and the area is cut off from its source of oxygen. In a relatively short period of time, the affected area dies and is no longer able to function. Depending upon the location within the brain, the individual who suffered the stroke may exhibit changes in personality, loss of memory, or the inability to function mentally as he or she did prior to the stroke.

Less obvious but just as devastating is multi-infarct dementia. Though not resulting from a large-scale stroke, multi-infarct dementia occurs following a series of "mini-strokes" in which very small areas of the brain are cut off from their source of oxygen. Because these occur at such a microscopic level, multiple "mini-strokes" can occur without being detected. Over time the accumulation of several affected areas can result in behavior characteristic of other forms of dementia.

By far, however, the most common form of dementia is Alzheimer's Disease (AD).[13] An estimated 70% of all cases of dementia are the result of AD.[14] Though it is possible to exhibit the characteristic signs of AD at an earlier age, most cases of AD occur later in life. In fact, 90% of all cases develop after the age of 65 with five out of every ten cases being seen in individuals over the age of 85.[15] In the past, an official diagnosis of AD was only possible with the results of an autopsy in which the presence of plagues and tangles in the neurons of the brain could be confirmed. However, the emergence of new medical tests now allow for a high rate of accuracy in diagnosing AD among persons who are still living.

Individuals with AD typically proceed through a

series of stages that involve the gradual deterioration of their mental capacities. A person with AD will typically experience the following[16]:

- decline in memory, attention, learning, and judgment
- difficulty in expressing oneself verbally
- confusion and disorientation
- decline in personal hygiene and self-care skills
- changes in personality
- inappropriate social behavior

Initially, the characteristic symptoms of AD are only minor and may seem to be the result of another psychological problem such as depression or delirium. For instance, a person who has been a meticulous money manager begins to lose track of significant sums of money. A woman who has prepared hundreds of meals for people who have been guests in her home cannot remember how to prepare a pot of coffee. The once outgoing, personable gentleman becomes easily agitated and very combative. Over time these initial symptoms become more intense and other conditions may be added as the AD patient moves into the more advanced stages of the disease.

Although AD is currently irreversible and incurable, medical and therapeutic interventions are available. A few prescription drugs have met with modest success in improving cognitive functions or behavioral difficulties. But even when these medications are fully effective they are not providing a cure for AD; they are simply helping to manage the consequences of the disease. Similarly, "reality orientation" has proven to be a useful means of managing an AD patient. Reality orientation is a form of therapy in which individuals with AD are constantly reminded of their name, the date, and where they are. The continual reinforcement of these basic pieces of information helps AD patients to connect to their immediate surroundings in the short-term. Like prescription medications, however, reality orientation does not alter the long-term progression of the disease.[17]

Implications for Ministry

Psychological changes are a normal part of the aging process. Relatively minor modifications in information processing, storage, and retrieval are seen quite commonly and should not be interpreted as being unusual. We should bear in mind, though, that every individual will experience these changes in different ways and the progression of the alterations will vary from one person to another. The presence of the various forms of dementia, especially Alzheimer's Disease, should be seen as an abnormal part of the aging process and one that will not affect the majority of senior adults. With this information in mind, there are two practical implications for ministry.

First, senior adults can continue to learn new things. When introducing new material, however, keep in mind the biological changes presented in Chapter 7, as well as the information in this chapter about memory. The size and color of the font in printed material is important as is the layout of the room where it is presented. Also, the time needed to store and retrieve the new information in memory may take slightly longer for senior adults. Rather than overwhelming the group with too much information, create a pace that allows for frequent repetition of the new material. If you are not sure of the appropriate pace, then ask the group for feedback and adjust your presentation based on their response. This method will help to create a more inclusive environment in which people from all age groups feel that they are welcomed to actively participate.

The second implication for ministry involves respite care. Though AD only afflicts 10% of the population over the age of 65, once the disease begins its progression it can continue for as long as twenty years.[18] During that time the burden of caring for the individual with AD is often assumed by a family member, typically a spouse, daughter, or daughter-in-law. As the disease moves into its more advanced stages, the caregiving responsibilities continue to mount and frequently take a toll on the health of the caregiver. Despite the negative consequences, the primary caregiver often continues providing the majority of care and refuses to consider other alternatives such as a nursing home. While the commitment to their loved one is noble, the caregiving responsibilities eventually reach a level that exceeds the ability of a single person.

As the responsibilities increase, an extremely valuable form of ministry to a caregiver and their family is to provide regularly scheduled periods of respite. Even if it consists of only a few hours a week, a caregiver needs time away from the physical and emotional responsibilities of daily care. During the early stages of AD, the duties of the respite care provider will typically be modest and may include visiting with the individual affected by AD. As the disease progresses respite care providers will benefit from becoming more informed about AD and the type of behavior that can be expected. Information of this type can be obtained by reading books such as *The 36 Hour Day*,[19] gathering information on AD via the Internet, or contacting the nearest chapter of the Alzheimer's Association.

Nine

The Sociology of Aging

As a group today's senior adults are the healthiest, most active, and well financed ever to live in the United States. In the midst of the abundance, however, the extent to which individual senior adults are sharing in the prosperity varies greatly. In this chapter we will examine the living arrangements and economic conditions of senior adults in our nation. We will also introduce the "aging network" in order to gain a better understanding of the programs and services available to senior adults, including Social Security and Medicare.

Living Arrangements

Until the latter part of the twentieth century, senior adult housing consisted of a limited number of options. The majority of senior adults lived either in their own home or in the residence of one of their adult children. For those who were unable to care for themselves or did not have a family member who could assist them, a nursing home was the only alternative. Although this pattern remains the predominate one in certain parts of the country, senior adult housing options have grown, with remaining in a personal residence or moving to a nursing home being the two extremes. In between are a variety of choices including independent living apartments, assisted living, and continuing care retirement communities. The number of housing alternatives other than a nursing home has increased so substantially that only 5% of senior adults live in a nursing home at any point in time.[1]

While senior adult living arrangements have become more diverse, one characteristic of senior adult households has remained fairly stable. Nearly one in four senior adult females live alone compared to one in twenty senior adult males.[2] The most reasonable explanation for this pattern is the fact that men tend to marry younger women and that women outlive men by approximately seven years. The result is that a far greater number of widows than widowers are found in senior adult groups. Another contributing factor is that a man has a greater chance of remarrying following the death of his spouse because the ratio of senior adult men to women is seven to ten among people between the ages of 65 and 84 and four to ten among those over the age of 85.[3]

As interesting as the demographic information is, of far greater concern are the ramifications of this pattern. Following the death of a spouse, many senior adults experience not only a period of intense grief but a significant shift in their living patterns as well. The loss of income that often accompanies the death of a spouse frequently requires the surviving member of the couple to reconsider their living arrangements. For those who choose to remain in their home, a new set of responsibilities often emerge such as cooking meals and cleaning the house for a male or maintaining the dwelling and managing the financial aspects of home ownership for a female. A responsive senior adult ministry will recognize the shift in domestic duties and will provide support and assistance during this time.

Social Security and Medicare

Prior to the establishment of the Social Security Administration in 1935, senior adults in the United States had very few financial options available to them. The predominant philosophy during the early years of the twentieth century was that individuals had the primary responsibility for their own well-being. For the poor, there was little sympathy. Their destitution was seen as being a just reward for the laziness or wastefulness that must have characterized their earlier years. Following the Great Depression, this ultra conservative philosophy changed dramatically as millions of Americans understood through personal experience that one's economic situation was not always as controllable as it was once thought to be. In response President Roosevelt's New Deal immersed the federal government into a process of economic recovery that continues to impact Americans in the twenty-first century.

Without a doubt the passage of the Social Security Act in 1935 was the single most significant component of the New Deal for senior adults. Based on a German model begun in the nineteenth century, Social Security originally had two parts. The first aspect of the program was designed to provide immediate relief for senior adults who were poor. Known as "Aid to the Aged," this part of Social Security was ended in 1972 and replaced with the Supplemental Security Income (SSI) program that is in place today.[4] SSI guarantees a minimum amount of monthly income for all senior adults even if they have not contributed to Social Security.

The second part of the Social Security Act established a long-term retirement program designed to provide a stable source of income to senior adults in future years. Originally known as "Old Age Insurance," the program has been renamed and is now referred to as "Old Age and Survivors, Disability, and Hospital Insurance" (OAS-DHI). Unlike SSI which is awarded to low-income persons, Social Security is based on contributions to the Social Security Trust Fund through the Federal Insurance Contributions Act (FICA). For individuals who are not self-employed, 7.65% of their gross wages are deducted by their employer and sent to Social Security. Their employer is also required to match the contribution so that approximately 15% of each employee's gross wages are being contributed to Social Security. Individuals who are self-employed must pay both the employee and employer's share of the deduction.

An individual becomes eligible for Social Security retirement benefits once he or she has accumulated 40 units of credit.[5] Since each calendar year consists of four quarters, a person typically becomes eligible to receive a retirement benefit after completing ten years of employment that has included regular contributions to Social

Security. The actual amount of one's retirement income varies according to their level of earnings and the age at which they choose to retire. Presently, full retirement benefits are available beginning at age 65 with a reduced benefit option being available at age 62. For persons born between 1943 and 1954, full benefits will not be available until age 66. Individuals born in 1960 or later will not be eligible to receive a full Social Security retirement benefit until the age of 67.[6] The gradual increase in the age at which full benefits become available is an attempt to stabilize the future of the Social Security system.

In combination with the income feature, Social Security also includes a health care component known as Medicare. Since its inception in 1965, Medicare has been providing health insurance to millions of senior adults. As a general rule individuals who are eligible for Social Security benefits are also eligible for Medicare Part A (hospital insurance). Part B of Medicare provides additional medical coverage but requires a person to pay a supplemental monthly fee.

Some senior adults also have access to another government-funded health care program known as Medicaid. An important distinction between the programs is that Medicaid is designed for needy individuals, which can include senior adults, and is subject to an income test. Another important difference is that Medicare is a federally-funded program while Medicaid is financed by federal and state dollars and is administered by state governments. The result is that Medicare is a uniform program across the country while Medicaid programs can vary from state to state.

Although the future of Social Security continues to be debated, the significance of the program to senior adults cannot be overstated.[7] Though it was never intended to be the only source of retirement income, for 63% of senior adults it is the major source of retirement income and for 25% it is the only form of income they have in their later years.[8] With the average monthly benefit being $765, those who rely exclusively on Social Security in their later years often live a precarious existence and have little room in their monthly budget for unexpected expenses.[9]

The Aging Network

The aging network consists of the programs and services available to senior adults that are funded by federal, state, and local sources. Though the Social Security system (1935) was one of the earliest components of the aging network, a full-scale response to the concerns of senior adults did not begin until the passage of the Older Americans Act in 1965. A significant part of the Older Americans Act was the establishment of the Administration on Aging (AoA) and the subsequent commitment to provide on-going funding in order to meet the needs of senior adults.

Using funds appropriated by Congress, the AoA distributes resources to state units on aging who in turn divide them among their respective Area Agencies on Aging (AAA). Each of the approximately 670 AAA across the nation serve as a clearinghouse for information, programs, and services for senior adults in a designated geographic area.[10] Because the funding mechanism is based on the number of people served, AAA in urban areas typically cover a much smaller geographic area than those in rural locations.

The actual programs and services that are available through an AAA will vary, though they are guided by several initiatives known as "titles." Title III, for instance, is the largest of the initiatives and focuses on the preparation and delivery of nutritionally balanced meals. Individuals 60 years of age or older can eat free either by visiting a senior center or by requesting that a meal be delivered to their home. Other titles emphasize education and research, programs for minority group individuals, and programs designed to counter elder abuse, neglect, and exploitation. The actual amount of available funds is determined periodically when the Older Americans Act is re-authorized by Congress and signed by the President. As certain areas increase or diminish in importance, adjustments are made in the allocation of dollars to specific titles.

In most cases the AAA is not directly involved in delivering programs or services. Instead, it is the point at which senior adults and their family members gain access to the wide range of offerings available to them through the aging network. As a result the AAA is an excellent place to begin in the search for answers about issues of interest to senior adults.

Implications for Ministry

One of the most useful ways to minister to, and with, senior adults is to become knowledgeable of the programs and services in the aging network. While it is not necessary to become an expert on the national trends or shifting policy debates, understanding how the aging network functions in your geographic area and becoming a resource person for members of your congregation will be invaluable to senior adults and their families. With a minimum investment of time, a "senior adult resource sheet" can be assembled with the names and phone numbers of key individuals in the aging network such as the director of the AAA and the local Social Security office. This information can be found in the white pages of the phone book or through directory assistance. Many AAA also have a website that can be accessed initially through the AoA homepage at www.aoa.gov. By following the "aging related web sites" link near the bottom of the page and then selecting "state and area agencies on aging," one can locate the AAA responsible for any geographic region in the country.

Another option is to invite staff members from the aging network to make a presentation during the regular meetings of the senior adult group and to allow time for a question and answer session at the end of the formal presentation. The presentation should include not only the benefits that can be received by senior adults but also the numerous ways in which senior adults can become involved in the community through volunteer or employment opportunities.

Ten

Implications for the 21st Century

As we enter the twenty-first century, many challenges and opportunities will be placed before the local church. Though many of these are unknown to us at the present time, the demographic realities of our population allow us to see one significant reality that will occur. In the absence of a significant surge of younger adults into local congregations, the majority of churches will experience a "graying" of their membership.

Far from being a negative event, however, this demographic shift can be an extremely positive transition as long as we are willing to embrace the new model of senior adult ministry. Congregations that maintain a mindset of ministry TO senior adults without incorporating ministry WITH senior adults will gradually diminish in size as their members "age in place." However, as congregations increasingly adopt the new model of ministry WITH senior adults, they will discover new opportunities for outreach, service, and spiritual growth.

In light of the changing demographics and the impact they will have on churches, the primary purpose of this book has been to provide the scriptural basis and strategic elements necessary to understand the need for adopting a new view of senior adults and ministry with them. Seeing senior adults as more than just passive recipients of ministry is an important point of departure in the movement toward acceptance and implementation of the new model. The largest portion of this transition will have to occur within the local congregation as the ministry staff, elders, and deacons provide direction and leadership to the members. However, other individuals and institutions will be active players in this process, particularly through the development of resource materials for current and prospective church leaders.

Preparing Future Ministers

A number of researchers have studied ministry student's knowledge of the aging process and their perceptions of the elderly. The results of the studies are very clear. People preparing to enter the ministry are poorly informed about the processes and realities of aging.[1] Several explanations have been offered for the absence of an age-based curriculum in ministry preparation programs. Chief among them is the challenge of finding time to teach a gerontology course without diminishing the focus on textual-based courses. While this is a valid argument, it should be kept in mind that many schools do offer specialized courses in areas such as youth ministry and family ministry. This suggests that other explanations for the absence of gerontology courses, such as the lack of faculty expertise or the lack of student interest, may be at the heart of the problem.

In order to raise awareness of the growing importance of senior adult ministry, and to fill the void until gerontology is considered a vital component of the ministry curriculum, several steps can be taken. First, guest lecturers can be invited to speak to students who are preparing to enter the ministry. The speakers can be faculty members from other academic departments in which aging courses are taught or members of the community with a recognized specialty in gerontology.

Second, Bible professors can include assignments within their existing courses that require students to read about issues that affect the elderly and relate them to ministry within a local congregation. They can also assign students to regularly visit an older person in order to develop a more realistic understanding of the realities that can accompany the later years.

Finally, ministry students can be encouraged to enroll in a basic course on aging such as "Introduction to Social Gerontology" or "The Sociology of Aging." Courses such as these typically provide a broad survey of the field of gerontology and cover issues such as life course development, the biological and psychological changes in aging, and the basic operation of programs such as Social Security and Medicare.

Continuing Education for Church Leaders

For those who have completed their formal education and are now involved in leadership positions within a local congregation, a different approach will be necessary.

Rather than focusing on credit bearing courses within a college or university, a more flexible method will be needed. An excellent venue in which to introduce the concept of ministry with senior adults is the lectureship setting. A session that addressed the growing importance of senior adult ministry and described the process of developing a ministry with senior adults would be a valuable addition to the program.

A second option for continuing education involves bringing a speaker to a local congregation. The obvious advantage of this option is that the entire congregation, rather than a handful of individuals, can be introduced to senior adult ministry. The guest speaker's presentations can serve as the foundation for an entire day or weekend dedicated to celebrating the role of the senior adults in the congregation and committing the church to ministry with them. In order for this to happen, the key points in the presentation should be delivered to a combined adult Bible class on Sunday morning followed by a sermon on the same topic during the worship service. Additional sessions focusing on topics like caregiving, senior adult housing, and Social Security can be offered during a more casual Friday night or Saturday morning gathering.

A third possibility involves accessing the offerings available through existing programs like the Pruett Gerontology Center (PGC), the Center for Aging, Religion, and Spirituality (CARS), the Center on Aging and Older Adult Ministries, or the Institute of Gerontological Studies at Baylor University. A brief description of each program is provided below with contact information listed in Appendix A.

As a part of Abilene Christian University, the Pruett Gerontology Center offers college courses leading to a degree in gerontology. However, the mission of the PGC extends beyond traditional academic boundaries. Each summer the PGC hosts the "Older Adult Ministry Conference." Over a span of three days church members and leaders gather to exchange information and ideas about senior adult ministry, share success stories, and encourage one another in their efforts to minister with senior adults.

The Center for Aging, Religion, and Spirituality is a part of Luther Seminary in St. Paul, Minnesota. Under the direction of Mel Kimble, it provides an interfaith and multi-disciplinary approach to issues related to aging, religion, and spirituality. The goals of CARS include providing academic and continuing education for individuals involved in ministry, encouraging scholarly research and providing an outlet for publication of research findings. Each summer CARS sponsors a two-week Geriatric Pastoral Care Institute that focuses on spirituality in later life as well as other social and health-related issues pertinent to senior adults and those who minister with them.

The Center on Aging and Older Adult Ministries was established by the General Board of Discipleship of The United Methodist Church in the fall of 2000. The Center was founded on the principle that faith development is a lifelong process and is critical for transforming the world. In order to assist individuals and churches in reaching this goal, the center provides a wide range of resources, including books, training support, networking opportunities, and assistance with research efforts.

Faculty members in the Institute of Gerontological Studies at Baylor University in Waco, Texas, have recently developed an on-line training course entitled, "A Higher Vision in Senior Adult Ministry." The course is an affordable, self-paced learning experience designed for those who want to learn more about ministry with senior adults but do not have the time or money to enroll in a college course.

A fourth option involves reading about senior adult ministry. Individuals or churches that are just beginning to consider the possibility of an organized senior adult ministry may choose to read printed material on the subject before traveling to a conference or bringing a speaker to their town. Unfortunately, the number of books and magazine articles dealing with senior adult ministry is limited (see Appendix A for a list of available resources). The material currently available is helpful, but researchers and ministers who are capable of writing informed pieces about senior adult ministry must become more active in order to share their knowledge with those who are new to the area.

Conclusion

The growing presence of senior adult Christians is opening the door to an exciting new era of ministry. While this book has focused on the emergence of a new model of ministry WITH senior adults, it must be understood that an effective senior adult ministry cannot exist in a vacuum. Specialized ministries for senior adults, college students, or young people can be beneficial in that they provide an opportunity for persons to connect to the church. An inherent danger in this approach, however, is that members can begin to identify more with their sub-group than the entire body resulting in an age-segregated church. To counter the potential for fragmentation, churches must create an atmosphere that values the contributions of each member of the church, irrespective of his or her age, in order to strengthen the entire body and nullify the negative myths and stereotypes between the generations. Due to their life experiences and knowledge of the Word, senior adult Christians can take the lead in this effort by committing themselves to developing intergenerational relationships and activities.[2]

In Romans 12:4-5 Paul says, "Just as each of us has one body with many members, and these members do not all have the same function, so in Christ we who are many form one body, and each member belongs to all the others." Each ministry can benefit the group for which it is primarily designed but ultimately it must contribute to the strengthening of the body. With its emphasis on ministry WITH senior adults rather than just TO them, the new model for senior adult ministry can serve as the platform upon which a strong intergenerational church can be built.

Chapter Notes

Chapter 1

1. Macionis, J. J. (2002). *Society: The basics* (6th ed.). Upper Saddle River, NJ: Prentice Hall, p. 77.

2. Palen, J. J. (2001). *Social problems for the twenty-first century*. Boston, MA: McGraw-Hill, p. 300.

3. Ibid, p. 300.

4. Taeuber, C. M., & Rosenwaike, I. (1992). A demographic portrait of America's Oldest Old. In R. Suzman, D. Willis, & K. Manton (Eds.), *The oldest old*. New York: Oxford University Press, p. 21.

5. Palen, J. J. (2001), p. 300.

6. Dychtwald, K. (1990). *Age wave*. New York: Bantam Books.

7. Thorson, J. A. (2000). *Aging in a changing society* (2nd ed.). Philadelphia, PA: Taylor & Francis Group, p. 30.

8. Dychtwald, K. (1990), p. 16.

9. Barrow, G. M. (1996). *Aging, the individual, and society* (6th ed.). Minneapolis/St. Paul, MN: West Publishing, p. 6.

10. Gelfand, D. E. (1999). *The aging network: Programs*

and services. New York: Springer Publishing, p. 3.

11. The figure is based on results from survey research of the Churches of Christ and Southern Baptist Convention combined with data provided by the Presbyterian Church (U.S.A) and the Lutheran Church (Missouri Synod). Information about the Episcopal Church is based on data from the *Journal of Religious Gerontology,* 13(1), 79.

12. Thorson, J. A. (2000). *Aging in a changing society,* p. 52.

13. The "new model" for senior adult ministry first appeared in the academic literature during the 1980s. Since then, a growing number of research articles and books have been written. Though several scholars and practitioners have contributed to the growth, James Ellor, Melvin Kimble, Harold Koenig, James Seeber, and Henry C. Simmons have been key figures in calling for a new way of thinking about ministry with senior adults. For additional information on the emergence of the new model for senior adult ministry, see the following:

Arn, W., & Arn, C. (1993). *Catch the age wave.* Grand Rapids, MI: Baker Book House.

Beal, D. P. (1982). Effective church ministry with older adults. *Journal of Christian Education,* 3, 5-17.

Carlson, D. (1997). *Engaging in ministry with older adults.* Bethesda, MD: Alban Institute.

Doka, K. (1985-1986). The church and the elderly: The impact of changing age strata on congregations. *International Journal of Aging and Human Development,* 22, 291-300.

Ellor, J. W., & Coates, R. B. (1986). Examining the role of the church in the aging network. J*ournal of Religion and Aging,* 2(1&2), 99-116.

Gallagher, D. P. (2002). *Senior adult ministry in the 21st century: Step-by-step strategies for reaching people over 50.*

Loveland, CO: Group Publishing, Inc.

Gentzler, R. H., Jr. (1999). *Designing an older adult ministry*. Nashville, TN: Discipleship Resources.

Kimble, M., & McFadden, S. (2002). *Aging, spirituality, and aging* (Vol. 2). Minneapolis, MN: Augsburg Fortress Press.

Koenig, H. G., Lamar, T., & Lamar, B. (1997). *A gospel for the mature years: Finding fulfillment by knowing and using your gifts*. New York: Haworth Pastoral Press.

Seeber, J. J. (1990). *Spiritual maturity in the later years*. New York: Haworth Pastoral Press.

Oliver, D. B. (2001). Reflections on the role of the church, synagogue, or parish in developing effective ministries with older persons. In D. R. Watkins (Ed.), *Religion and aging: An anthology of the Poppele papers* (pp. 37-43). New York: Haworth Pastoral Press.

Simmons, H. C., & Wilson, J. (2001). Soulful aging: Ministry through the stages of adulthood. Marion, GA: Smyth & Helwys Publishing.

Tobin, S., Ellor, J., & Anderson, Ray S. (1986). *Enabling the elderly: Religious institutions within the community service system*. Albany: State University Press of New York.

Chapter 2

1. The word study was conducted with *PC Study Bible*, Version 3 for Windows. Published by Bible Soft, Seattle, WA. All scripture references are based on the *New International Version*.

2. Several different Hebrew terms relate to aging including: *zaqen* – a designation of advanced age or an indication of nobility (see for instance Gen. 24:1-2, 25:8, 47:28, 50:7, Num. 22:7, 2 Sam. 12:17).

seba – a synonym for aging meaning "gray head" (see for instance 1 Chron. 29:28, Prov. 16:31, Dan. 7:9).

yases – an aged and decrepit person (2 Chron. 36:17) .

yasis – worthy of respect due to one's age (Job 15:10, 32:6).

3. In the New Testament, *geras* or *gerasko* refer to old age in general (see for instance Luke 1:36, Heb. 8:13). *Presbytes* is the New Testament term for elder and is frequently used to describe the leadership of a group of people (see for instance Luke 1:18, Philemon 9, 1 Tim 5:1-2, Titus 2:2-3).

For additional information, see Elwell, W. A. (1996). *Baker theological dictionary of the Bible.* Grand Rapids, MI: Baker Books, and Harris, J. G. (1987). *Biblical perspectives on aging: God and the elderly.* Minneapolis, MN: Fortress Press.

4. The Bible also includes several passages that address the treatment of widows including Deut. 24:19-21, 26:12-13, 27:19; Jeremiah 7:6, 22:3; and 1 Tim. 5:5-9.

5. Due to physical and mental limitations some individuals will need, primarily, to be ministered to. However, the vast majority of individuals in a congregation should seek to identify their God-given gift and use it in service to Him by serving others.

Chapter 4

1. Bee, H. L. (2000). *The journey of adulthood* (4th ed.). Upper Saddle River, NJ: Prentice Hall, pp. 342-344.

Chapter 6

1. Thornton, J. A. (1998). *I was a sky pilot.* Henderson, TN: Hester Publications.

2. Macular degeneration is a disease that affects the central vision of an individual. The presence of macular degeneration impacts the ability of the individual to distinguish the finer details of an object that is being viewed. Source: Spence, A. P. (1999). *Biology of human aging* (2nd ed.). Upper Saddle River, NJ: Prentice Hall.

Chapter 7

1. See for instance:

Djupe, A. M., & Westberg, G. (1995). Congregation-based health programs. In M. A. Kimble, S. H. McFadden, J. W. Ellor, & J. J. Seeber (Eds.), *Aging, spirituality, and religion* (pp. 325-334). Minneapolis, MN: Fortress Press.

Ellor, J. W., & Bracki, M. A. (1995). Assessment, referral, and networking. In M. A. Kimble, S. H. McFadden, J. W. Ellor, & J. J. Seeber (Eds.), *Aging, spirituality, and religion* (pp. 148-160). Minneapolis, MN: Fortress Press.

2. See for instance:

Brewer, E. D. C. (1989). A national study of gerontology in theological education. In B. Payne & E. D. C. Brewer (Eds.), *Gerontology in theological education* (pp. 15-25). New York: Haworth Press.

Carlson, R. W. (1985). The Episcopal seminaries and aging: A survey of Episcopal seminaries and schools of theology as to teaching and training in the field of ministry to the aged. *Journal of Religion and Aging*, 1(4), 1-11.

Knapp, J. L., & Beaver, L. M., & Reed, T. D. (2002). Perceptions of the elderly among ministers and ministry students: Implications for seminary curricula. *Educational Gerontology*, 28(4), 1-12.

Pieper, H. G., & Garrison, T. (1992). Knowledge of social aspects of aging among pastors. *Journal of Religious Gerontology*, 8(4), 89-105.

Sheehan, N. W., Wilson, R., & Marella, L. M. (1988). The role of the church in providing services for the aging. *Journal of Applied Gerontology*, 7(2), 231-241.

3. Quadagno, J. (1999). *Aging and the life course*. Boston, MA: McGraw-Hill, p. 128.

4. Spence, A. P. (1999). *Biology of human aging* (2nd ed.). Upper Saddle River, NJ: Prentice Hall, p. 40.

5. Carroll, D. L. (1989). *When your loved one has Alzheimer's: A caregiver's guide.* New York: Harper & Row, p. 91.

6. Bee, H. L. (2000). *The journey of adulthood* (4th ed.). Upper Saddle River, NJ: Prentice Hall, p. 71.

7. Spence, A. P. (1999). *Biology of human aging* (2nd ed.). p. 100.

8. Ibid, p. 102

9. Ibid, p. 103

10. Bee, H. L. (2000). *The journey of adulthood* (4th ed.). p. 72.

11. Spence, A. P. (1999). Biology of human aging (2nd ed.), p. 106-107.

12. Ibid, p. 107

13. Ibid, p. 52.

14. Quadagno, J. (1999). *Aging and the life course*, p. 132.

15. Bee, H. L. (2000). *The journey of adulthood* (4th ed.), p. 74.

16. Spence, A. P. (1999). Biology of human aging (2nd ed.), p. 59.

17. Bee, H. L. (2000). The journey of adulthood (4th ed.), p. 76.

18. Quadagno, J. (1999). *Aging and the life course*, p. 136.

19. Spence, A. P. (1999). Biology of human aging (2nd ed.), p. 125.

Chapter 8

1. Quadagno, J. (1999). *Aging and the life course.* Boston, MA: McGraw-Hill, p. 152.

2. Bee, H. L. (2000). *The journey of adulthood* (4th ed.). Upper Saddle River, NJ: Prentice Hall, p. 136.

3. Ibid, p. 136.

4. Cavanaugh, J. C., & Blanchard-Fields, F. (2002). *Adult development and aging* (4th ed.). Belmont, CA: Wadsworth, p. 215.

5. Ibid, p. 179.

6. Ibid, p. 215.

7. Ibid, p. 212.

8. Quadagno, J. (1999). Aging and the life course, p. 153.

9. Bee, H. L. (2000). The journey of adulthood (4th ed.), p. 138.

10. Cavanaugh, J. C., & Blanchard-Fields, F. (2002). *Adult development and aging* (4th ed.), p. 214.

11. Spence, A. P. (1999). *Biology of human aging* (2nd ed.), p. 89.

12. Cavanaugh, J. C., & Blanchard-Fields, F. (2002). *Adult development and aging* (4th ed.), p. 123.

13. Blazer, D. (1998). *Emotional problems in later life* (2nd ed.). New York: Springer, p. 36.

14. Fromholt, P., & Bruhn, P. (1999). Cognitive dysfunction and dementia. In I. H. Nordhus, G. R. VandenBos, S. Berg, & P. Fromholt (Eds.), *Clinical geropsychology* (pp. 183-188). Washington, DC: American Psychological Association.

15. Bee, H. L. (2000). *The journey of adulthood* (4th ed.), p. 107.

16. Quadagno, J. (1999). *Aging and the life course*, p. 153.

17. Ibid, p. 155.

18. Bee, H. L. (2000). *The journey of adulthood* (4th ed.), p. 110.

19. Mace, N., & Rabins, P. (1981). *The 36-hour day : A family guide for persons with Alzheimer's Disease, related dementing illnesses, and memory loss in later life*. Baltimore, MD: John Hopkins University Press.

Chapter 9

1. Quadagno, J. (1999). *Aging and the life course.* Boston, MA: McGraw-Hill, p. 69.

2. McLaughlin, D. K., & Jensen, L. (1998). The rural elderly: A demographic portrait. In R. T. Coward and J. A Krout (eds.), *Aging in rural settings: Life circumstances and distinctive features* (pp. 15-43), New York: Springer Publishing.

3. Ibid, p. 22.

4. Thorson, J. A. (2000). *Aging in a changing society* (2nd ed.). Philadelphia, PA: Taylor & Francis Group, p. 377.

5. Gelfand, D. E. (1999). T*he aging network: Programs and services.* New York: Springer Publishing Co., p. 31.

6. Thorson, J. A. (2000). Aging in a changing society (2nd ed.), p. 380.

7. Since its passage in 1935, Social Security has expanded and now includes several additional programs such as spouse benefits, survivor's benefits, and disability insurance.

8. Mooney, L. A., Knox, D., & Schacht, C. (2000). *Understanding social problems* (2nd ed.). Belmont, CA: Wadsworth/ Thompson Learning, p. 155.

9. Thorson, J. A. (2000). Aging in a changing society (2nd ed.), p. 378.

10. Krout, J. A. (1998). Services and service delivery in rural environments. In R. T. Coward and J. A Krout (eds.), *Aging in rural settings: Life circumstances and distinctive features* (pp. 247-266), New York: Springer Publishing.

Chapter 10

1. Knapp, J. L., & Elder, J. (2002). Infusing gerontological content into theological education. *Educational Gerontology,* 28(3), 1-11.

2. For additional information on intergenerational relationships in a church setting see:

Harkness, A. G. (1998). Intergenerational education for an intergenerational church? *Religious Education*, 93, 431-447.

Harkness, A. G. (1998). Intergenerational Christian education: An imperative for effective education in local churches (Part 1). *Journal of Christian Education*, 41(2), 5-14.

Harkness, A. G. (1998). Intergenerational Christian education: An imperative for effective education in local churches (Part 2). *Journal of Christian Education*, 42(1), 37-50.

Icenogle, G. W. (1994). *Biblical foundations for small group ministry: An intergenerational approach.* Downers Grove, IL: InterVarsity Press.

Prest, E. (1993). *From one generation to another.* Capetown: Training for Leadership.

White, J. W. (1988). *Intergenerational religious education.* Birmingham, AL: Religious Education Press.

Appendix A

Articles & Books

Arn, W., & Arn, C. (1993). *Catch the age wave.* Grand
Rapids, Michigan: Baker Book House.

Beal, D. P. (1982). Effective church ministry with older
adults. *Journal of Christian Education, 3,* 5-17.

Bentley, V. (1999). *Glory days: 366 daily readings for
mature Christians.* Dallas, TX: Bentley Books.

Carlson, D. (1997). *Engaging in ministry with older
adults.* Bethesda, MD: Alban Institute.

Carlson, D., & Seicol, S. (1990, Fall). Adapting worship to
changing needs. *Generations,* 65-66.

Clements, W. M. (1989). *Ministry with the aging: Designs,
challenges, and foundations.* New York: Haworth Press.

Doka, K. (1985-1986). The church and the elderly: The
impact of changing age strata on congregations. *International Journal of Aging and Human Development,*
22, 291-300.

Ellor, J. W., & Coates, R. B. (1986). Examining the role of
the church in the aging network. *Journal of Religion*

and Aging, 2 (1 & 2), 99-116.

Gallagher, D. P. (2002). *Senior adult ministry in the 21st century: Step-by-step strategies for reaching people over 50.* Loveland, CO: Group Publishing, Inc.

Gentzler, R. H., Jr. (1999). *Designing an older adult ministry.* Nashville, TN: Discipleship Resources.

Harkness, A. G. (1998). Intergenerational education for an intergenerational church? *Religious Education,* 93, 431-447.

Harris, J. G. (1987). *Biblical perspectives on aging: God and the elderly.* Minneapolis, MN: Fortress Press.

Hendrickson, M. C. (1986). The role of the church in aging: Implications for policy and action. *Journal of Religion & Aging,* 12, 5-16.

Icenogle, G. W. (1994). *Biblical foundations for small group ministry: An intergenerational approach.* Downers Grove, IL: InterVarsity Press.

Kimble, M., & McFadden, S. (2002). *Aging, spirituality, and aging* (Vol. 2). Minneapolis, MN: Augsburg Fortress Press.

Knapp, J. L., & Elder, J. (2002). Infusing gerontological content into theological education. *Educational Gerontology,* 28 (3), 1-11.

Knapp, J. L., Beaver, L. M., & Reed, T. D. (2002). Perceptions of the elderly among ministers and ministry students: Implications for seminary curricula. *Educational Gerontology,* 28 (4), 1-12.

Knapp, J. L. (2001). The impact of congregation-related variables on programs for senior adult members. *Journal of Applied Gerontology,* 20 (1), 24-38.

Knapp, J., & Hughes, J. (1998). Responding to the needs

of aging church members: The case of a religious group in Texas. *Southwest Journal on Aging*, 14(2), 137-141.

Koenig, H. G., McCullough, M. E., & Larson, D. B. (2000). *Handbook of religion and health*. New York: Oxford University Press.

Koenig, H. G., Lamar, T., & Lamar, B. (1997). *A gospel for the mature years: Finding fulfillment by knowing and using your gifts*. New York: Haworth Press.

Nouwen, H. J., & Gaffney, W. J. (1990). *Aging: The fulfillment of life*. New York: Doubleday.

Oakes, C. G. (2000). *Working the gray zone: A call for proactive ministry by and with older adults*. Franklin, TN: Providence House Publishers.

Prest, E. (1993). *From one generation to another*. Capetown: Training for Leadership.

Seeber, J. J. (1990). *Spiritual maturity in the later years*. New York: Haworth Press.

Sheehan, N. W., Wilson, R., & Marella, L. M. (1988). The role of the church in providing services for the aging. *The Journal of Applied Gerontology*, 7 (2), 231-241.

Simmons, H. C., & Wilson, J. (2001). *Soulful aging: Ministry through the stages of adulthood*. Marion, GA: Smyth & Helwys Publishing.

Steinitz, L. Y. (1981). The local church as support for the elderly. *Journal of Gerontological Social Work*, 4(2), 43-53.

Stuckey, J. C. (1998). The church's response to Alzheimer's disease. *The Journal of Applied Gerontology*, 17 (1), 25-37.

Tobin, S. S., & Ellor, J. W. (1983, Fall). The church and the aging network: More interaction needed. *Generations*,

26-28.

Tobin, S., Ellor, J., & Anderson-Ray, S. (1986). *Enabling the elderly: Religious institutions within the community service system*. Albany: State University Press of New York.

Watkins, D. R. (2001). *Religion and aging: An anthology of the Poppele papers*. Binghamton, NY: Haworth Press.

White, J. W. (1988). *Intergenerational religious education*. Birmingham, AL: Religious Education Press.

Other Resources

CARS: The Center for Aging, Religion, and Spirituality.
Luther Seminary
2481 Como Avenue
St. Paul, MN 55108-1496
(651) 641-3581
www.aging-religion-spirituality.com

Center on Aging & Older Adult Ministries
P.O. Box 340003
Nashville, TN 37203-0003
(877) 899-2780 ext. 7173
www.aging-umc.edu

Hughes, J. "How to build a positive senior adult ministry in a church environment." Available for purchase by contacting Dr. Hughes at (214) 823-2179.

Institute of Gerontological Studies
Baylor University
P.O. Box 97292
Waco, TX 76798-7292
(254) 710-3701

Journal of Religious Gerontology
An interdisciplinary journal of practice, theory, and applied research. Available from The Haworth Press, Inc.
1-800-429-6784

Pruett Gerontology Center
ACU Box 27793
Abilene, TX 79699-7793
(915) 674-2350

Appendix B

Methodology

The information in this book is based on three separate studies conducted by the author. The first study took place in the spring of 1998, the second during the spring of 2001, and the third during the spring of 2002. Information about each study is presented below.

Spring, 1998

A systematic random sample was employed using Mac Lynn's book, *Churches of Christ in the United States* (1997 edition), as the sampling frame. If a congregation had a complete mailing address and more than 25 members, it was eligible for inclusion in the sample.

A cover letter and survey were mailed to the congregations in the sample and the pulpit minister was asked to complete the survey and return it in the enclosed, postage-paid envelope. The survey consisted of a variety of questions about the demographic composition of the congregation, as well as the programs and services that were available for senior adult members. A second mailing was sent to congregations that did not respond to the initial mailing. Although the same survey was sent, a different cover letter was included. Completed surveys were received from 754 congregations with the greatest number of responses coming from six states (Texas, Tennessee, Alabama, Arkansas, California, and Oklahoma).

Spring, 2001

The focus of the second study was on larger congregations. A modified version of the original survey was sent to every congregation with an average Sunday morning worship attendance of 300 or more. The 2000 edition of *Churches of Christ in the United States* was used to identify the sample.

A cover letter and survey were mailed to the congregations in the sample and the pulpit minister was asked to complete the survey and return it in the enclosed, postage-paid envelope. The survey consisted of a variety of questions about the demographic composition of the congregation, as well as the programs and services that were available for senior adult members. In addition, an open-ended question was included in which the respondent was asked to describe the senior adult ministry of the church, if one existed. This information was used to identify "well-developed" senior adult ministries and served as the basis for several in-depth interviews that took place over the telephone or in person.

Completed surveys were received from 255 congregations. Since the study focused on larger congregations, the majority of the responses were received from states in which Churches of Christ have a strong presence such as Texas, Tennessee, and Alabama.

Spring, 2002

A systematic random sample was employed using the *Directory of Southern Baptist Churches* (2000) as the sampling frame. A cover letter and survey were mailed to the congregations in the sample and the pastor was asked to complete the survey and return it in the enclosed, postage-paid envelope. The survey consisted of a variety of questions about the demographic composition of the congregation, as well as the programs and services that were available for senior adult members.

Completed surveys were received from 150 congregations. Though the phrase "Southern Baptist Church" suggests that it is restricted to a particular region of the country, responses were received from 26 different states.